The Lancashire and Yorkshire Railway around Preston

EUXTON, FARINGTON & PRESTON.

From Fleetwood
LEA ROAD

Fr. Lancaster
OXHEYS

P.&W. GOODS (MAUDLANDS)
P.&W. GOODS BRCH JN.

To Longridge

DEEPDALE PASS.
JUNCTION

GREEN BANK SID.

2m 45c
36c
30c
11c
0m 68c
2.4c
39c
19c
10c
DEEPDALE GOODS

RIBBLE BRANCH
1m 23c
DOCK
1m 30c
P.&W. JUNC.
P.&L. JUNC.
14c

DOCK STREET JN.

PRESTON

STRAND ROAD JUNCTION
JOINT PASS. & JN. (FISHERGATE)
BUTLER STREET GOODS (L.&Y.)

CHRISTIAN ROAD GOODS (L.&N.W.)
W. LANCS. GOODS STA.
JN.
39c
26c
25c
30c
JUNC.

R. RIBBLE

RIBBLE JUNCTION
0m 66c
1m 24c
33c
0m 26c
22c

PENWORTHAM JUNCTION
28c
MIDDLEFORTH JUNC.
23c
23c
28c
WHITEHOUSE JUNC.
0m 26c
0m 74c

From Southport

FARINGTON WEST JUNC.
8c
0m 58c
0m 37c
1m 0c
PRESTON JN. STA.
JUNCTION
9c
0m 49c
JUNCTION
37c
BAMBER BRIDGE STA.
To Blackburn
17c

30c
23.7c
0m 46c
JUNC.
COSTOCK HALL STA.
45c
EAST JUNC.

MOSS LANE JUNC.
55c PASS.
20c
18c
GOODS JUNC.

FARINGTON

1m 60c
1m 33c

MIDGE HALL

LEYLAND

From Liverpool

EXPLANATION

CORPORATION OF PRESTON	
LANCASHIRE & YORKSHIRE	
LONDON & NORTH WESTERN	
L.&Y. & L.&N.W. JOINT { NORTH UNION	
PRN & LONGRIDGE	
PRESTON & WYRE }	
N. UNION & CORPORATION JOINT	

EUXTON

JUNCTION 12c
L.&Y. STA.
To Bolton
1m 24c
To Wigan

BALSHAW LANE & EUXTON

The Lancashire and Yorkshire Railway around Preston

A history of the East and West Lancashire sections including Lostock Hall

Bob Gregson

ATKINSON PUBLICATIONS LTD

In memory of my dear parents,
John and Hilda Gregson

Cover illustrations:

Front cover: Fairburn tank, 42154, on the Ribble bridge with a local train for Southport.
(Stan Withers)

Back cover: Top, View of the East Lancashire station and yard from Vicar's Bridge in August 1959, with Austerity 90266 returning light to Lostock Hall shed.
(Ben Brookesbank)
Bottom, Britannia pacific, 70012 *John of Gaunt*, bereft of nameplates, reverses over the points across from the East Lancs Goods signal box, circa 1966.
(Peter Ditchfield)

Frontispiece: A 1913 diagram of Preston area junctions as published for the Railway Clearing House.

First published December 2011
Reprinted January 2012

Atkinson Publications Limited
18 Highgate, Goosnargh
Preston, Lancashire PR3 2BX
www.atkinsonspublications.co.uk

British Library Cataloguing in Publication Data.
A catalogue record for this book is available from the British Library.

ISBN 978 0 9565 1845 3

Typesetting and Origination by Atkinson Publications Limited.
Printed and bound by CPI Group (UK) Ltd, Croydon, CR0 4YY

Contents

Acknowledgements

I would like to take this opportunity to thank the following people for all their help without which the completion of this book would not have been possible.

First of all, my special thanks to Mike Norris who painstakingly provided me with much detailed information on working timetables, accident reports, facts, figures and nomenclature relating to signalling and track systems, and for his valuable assistance in rectifying computer problems.

Heather Crook, Mrs. Lilian Counsell MBE, Margaret Heyes, Adrian Bradshaw, Mike Atherton, Bob Tye, John Fletcher, Paul Tuson, Stan Withers, Jack Hodgkinson, Alan Castle, Bill Ashcroft, Jim Heron, David Hindle, Chris Spring, Arthur Haymes, Keith Till, Richard Kirkby, Peter Vickers, John Bargh, Brindle Historical Society, Dr. David Hunt, Ernie Tyrer, Mel Parker, Jeff Mimnagh, Ken Roberts, Andy Hall, Eric (Tom) Jones, Pete Whalen, Bob Gant, Vinny & John Commons, Brian Dodds, Walter (Rocky) Thompson, Noel Coates, Ted (Jacko) Jackson, Jim Marlor, Jim Walker, David & Sylvie Holmes, Dennis Westwood, Tommy Gorman, Norman Bullcock, Tony Gillett, Peter Rigby, Barry Frankland, Ivan Stewart, Tom Wray, Chris Canning, David Burdon, R.J.Essery, Colin Stacey, E. H. Wood, J .S. Hancock, Malcolm Baker, James Nevins, Paul Wood, John Rigby and many other Lostock Hall and Preston railwaymen, too numerous to mention.
The Harris Library and Museum, Lancashire Records Office, Greater Manchester Records Office, The National Railway Museum, National Grid Archives, National Records Office, British Railways Board, Lancashire County Council, Lancashire Evening Post, South Ribble Museum, Leyland Library.

In memoriam: Ada Ashworth, Barny and Terry Campbell, Bill Wilson, Richard Wilson, Bill Pollard, Cliff Morris, Ronnie Pye, Bert Stewart, Billy Jackson, Ernie Heyes, Keith Holding, Billy Bamber, Cliff Cornwell, Bernard Jacquier, Peter Ditchfield,

A gathering of retired Lancashire enginemen at the Ribble Steam Railway Museum on August 4th, 2010.
.... We have men here from Lostock Hall, Preston, Rose Grove and Carnforth. *(Alan Castle)*

Foreword

Some years ago I began gathering material together for a publication on the history and development of the railway infrastructure around Lostock Hall. As things progressed, however, I decided to expand the work to cover the long closed network of junctions and triangles of the former East and West Lancashire lines, including the stations at Butler Street and Fishergate Hill. The choice of title, although perhaps a little misleading, stems from the fact that all the railways focused upon in this book were absorbed into the Lancashire & Yorkshire Railway Company at one time or another. I have endeavoured to create a balance between the mechanical and structural side and the human element. For example, the problems, hazards and seemingly insurmountable obstacles which faced the civil engineers and navvies alike. The inclement weather, which hampered just about all of the below-mentioned construction work, often set the contracts back by many weeks, and was enough to test the patience and stamina of the strongest mortal. There was the on-going animosity between rival companies, which frequently left their clients in a state of confusion and distress; and the constant financial struggles of directors, share-holders and bankers regarding construction, development and operating costs, of which the latter continued to be the subject of all major issues with the private railway companies right up to the eve of nationalisation. Above all, there are the railwaymen and women who often had to work long and unsociable hours in a variety of adverse conditions to keep the wheels turning.

My own personal recollections go back to the journeys I made by train in the late 50's and throughout the following decade up to the end of steam traction in 1968. Growing up in a Lancashire mill town in the 1960's left its poignant and indelible marks, which are as clear to the mind today as they ever were. Following the stagnation of the preceding decade, the 60's was one of rapid change and marked the twilight years of the Victorian industrial legacy. The textile and allied engineering industries, which for so many decades had been the raison d'etre of the majority of East Lancashire towns, were now in decline. Many of the huge mills along the Blakewater valley stood silent, empty and derelict; bereft of all machinery and boilers, their tall chimneys little more than monuments to another age. Working class communities were breaking up, and those who had once been dependent on the local industries for a livelihood were moving on to other places, leaving behind them whole blocks of terraced houses with doorways and ground-floor windows bricked-up and awaiting the big hammer. Everywhere the air was thick with the stench of soot, dust and burning timbers from the demolition sites. Much of the local railway infrastructure was also in visible decline, and the freight service was diminishing together with the industries for which it was originally designed to serve. As time went on, fewer vehicles were to be seen in the goods yards, and some of the once numerous sidings were beginning to disappear beneath a tangle of undergrowth, with the rail tops covered in black rust.

It was all the more fascinating to me in those days as it appeared that very little had changed since the 19th century. For instance, most of the stations in the area remained gas-lit and retained much of their original architectural characteristics which included wrought-iron canopies, flagstone platforms, coal fires and separate waiting rooms for ladies and gentlemen, with one or two still sporting thick, plate-glass windows with the gender and class etched into them.

Although British Railways had replaced much of the signage with their maroon enamelled pressed steel designs, remnants of the old companies such as iron door-plates and wooden information boards with cast-iron capital letters remained in situ until the end. Among other survivors were the rust-caked iron signs which continued to remind the public to 'Beware of the Trains' with the 'Sum of Forty Shillings' being the price of trespass. The principles of mechanical signalling had remained much the same since the 1800's, with large iron lever frames, mahogany-cased block telegraph instruments and brass bells etc., all contained with the signalmen in draughty timber cabins. Most of the lamps used for signalling, locomotives and guarding duties were of the petroleum type with reservoirs, wicks and reflectors. Modern innovations were slow coming forward on the railways in the North-West, and for some parts it never came at all. Old traditions died hard and it seemed as though there was either a shortage of funding for modernisation, or that the railway men preferred to stick to the traditional tried, tested and reliable methods. The fact was, that in the wake of the Beeching report, it was not considered to be worthwhile up-grading secondary routes until positive decisions had been made regarding their future.

On the motive power scene, a few surviving pre-groupers struggled on up to 1962, and there was still a good variety of grouping locomotives from the 1920's through to the BR standard designs of the 50's, with Diesels still in the minority. LMS non-corridor stock continued to be used on local trains and notwithstanding the fact that the continuous braking system had been around for decades, there were still many loose-coupled or partially fitted freight trains on the main lines.

With the exception of mechanical coaling and ash plants, improved ablutions and lighting, little had changed over the decades in the day to day operations at the engine sheds or motive power depots as they were officially called. We still had fire-raisers, bar lads, fire-droppers (or disposal staff), boiler washers, boiler smiths, brick-arch builders, fitters, cleaners and yard labourers, all doing much the same type of work as their grandfathers had done. On my visits to Lostock Hall shed I came to realise what was expected of a young lad before he could become an engine driver. It didn't put me off the idea of wanting to become one (even though I was kidding myself into believing it was all going to be there waiting for me when I left school - which it wasn't), but it was an eye-opener. I got to see it all first-hand: shovelling ash out of a smoke box on a breezy day, lifting hot fire-bars out with giant iron tongues, dropping the fire and raking out the ash-pan; hosing-down the burning cinders and shovelling the steaming, acrid broth up-hill into a 10 ton truck. There was the coal-breaking, shovelling, prodding, oiling, sanding, lamp-trimming and later on, the pointless task of cleaning which, by the end of 1967, was left to a handful of enthusiastic volunteers. I will always remember a certain Saturday evening at the shed in the Winter of '65/'66. It was bitterly cold, with a fog bank moving in from the west. Each cast-iron water column had a fire-devil next to it and there were others here and there in the yard to prevent the points from freezing. Together with the smoke and steam from the engines and the larger than life shadows flitting about, it resembled a veritable presentiment of damnation, and had it not been for the faintly discernible introductory music for the BBC's Sport's Report programme wafting over from the offices across the way, one could have been forgiven for thinking the clock had gone back over seventy years.

I think the title for this stirring piece of music is called 'Out of the Blue'. It came out of a different colour that evening!

It all resembled something of a large-scale working museum, when compared to developments in and around London and the ultra-modern railway infrastructures of Western Europe. As youngsters we were under the impression that all this was being put on for our entertainment; the railwaymen, however, saw things in a different light: it was a job, with abnormal working patterns, hard graft and as much overtime as possible if an acceptable standard of living was to be attained. It had been just the same for their predecessors, and the only museum piece, as far as they were concerned, was the pay packet. Those in the Accounts Office at Euston and the disciples of Ernest Marples saw it all as a costly burden to the tax-payers, and by the mid 60's the well-schemed process of transferring people and goods from steel to tarmac was well underway.

For people like myself, the railway served as a form of escape, if only to get out into the country for a while before arriving at another burning mill town. What made these journeys to Preston, Southport and Ormskirk particularly interesting was the pleasant countryside through which the lines passed.

The most scenic, perhaps, was the route from Blackburn to Preston via Todd Lane Junction, which skirts the Darwen valley from Cherry Tree to Hoghton, giving spectacular views of the hills and wooded areas to the north of Pleasington, and the fertile, flat-lying countryside to the west.

The section from Whitehouse to Preston afforded equally beautiful views of the flood plain and pastureland, with the tree-lined formation of the old Walton Summit tram road in the background. On approaching Preston, the Ribble bridge provided a good vantage point for a panoramic view of Avenham and Millar parks, with the magnificent Park Hotel building over to the left; which looked particularly resplendent when the red brickwork and window panes glowed like fire in the early morning sunlight. It occasionally appeared like an apparition of Valhalla, when only the lofty tower and chimney stacks were clearly visible above the crimson-tinted river mist.

The arrival at Preston East Lancs. brought to an end any fancies folks might have been having on the journey. One awakened to the sights and sounds of a busy station: the slamming of carriage doors, a protracted, high-pitched note on a guard's whistle; a responsive hoot on a steam whistle followed by a loud, progressive pattern of exhaust blasts, drowning out the already unintelligible noise coming over the P.A. system. An anxious effort to catch a glimpse of the engine would occasionally be hampered by a detachment of people, freshly liberated from the confines of the carriages, hurrying past to catch the connection or get to work on time; and for a few seconds the engine fumes were diluted somewhat by a mixture of social fragrances in the form of cheap perfumes, hair oils, after-shaves, tobacco smoke and fusty garments. Over to the east side we watched the activity in Butler Street goods yard, and here we heard a slightly different kind of music: the discordant tympani of clashing buffer heads and the accompanying clink and rattle of coupling chains; the dull rumbling of moving goods vans and the piercing squeal of wheel flanges as they ground against the short-radiused curves and switches.

Now and then was heard the shriek of a steam whistle and the F-major blast of a shunter's horn, followed by the hiss of escaping steam and the hollow clank of coupling rods. Amid this infernal symphony of iron, steel and steam could be heard the comparatively feeble chords of the human voice, issuing orders, warnings and curses.

This was the tough and challenging world of the railway; a world of its own; an industry in itself, serving the needs of millions and itself in turn being served by an army of tens of thousands. It was a living creature without a soul, fashioned by the masters of mechanical and civil engineering; a bringer of stability and sustenance to the cautious, and merciless death and disaster to the careless. Never a slave to its creators, but always ready to pit itself against those who would be its masters. It incorporated a religion whose Bible was the company rule book and whose symbol was the ubiquitous time piece: a twenty four hour relentless icon, to whom both servants and served were dutifully committed.

Once all this fascinating and occasionally perverse activity had been witnessed and understood, one was more than likely to become an incurable enthusiast, possessing a love/hate relationship with a fast-disappearing epoch in mankind's progressive struggle to achieve total oblivion. As time went on there were fewer good days than bad, but I always went back for more. Our happy times on the station didn't last long, for within a few minutes the sinister figure of a platform inspector would emerge from the smoky shadows, heading towards us with a purposeful gait. We were then ordered off the premises, tickets or no tickets.

The count-down began in the early Summer of 1968, when the radius of steam activity was narrowed down to the North West, with just three steam sheds remaining: Carnforth, Lostock Hall and Rose Grove. One by one the steam locomotives were taken out of service and shunted onto the scrap sidings, leaving a handful to work the various 'end of steam' specials on Sunday August 4th. My last visit to Lostock Hall shed that year was on the morning of August 5th, which was a particularly sad occasion. The shed was little more than a graveyard: the dead engines were lined-up in rows, with one or two still warm from the previous night. We climbed up into the cab of an 8F, which still had some glowing embers on the grate. I remember throwing one or two cobs of coal into the firebox in a futile effort to prolong a life that had flickered-out forever a few hours before. We sat there for a while reminiscing and speculating on the future, during which time a familiar looking group of men, who were not readily recognisable in their casual clothing, left the boss's office for the last time, each carrying with him a brown envelope. Lostock Hall station closed a few days later, and within the following four years, the East Lancs. section from Bamber Bridge to Butler Street had closed. In those dark days of ruthless transition and rationalisation, I didn't leave the railway - it left me.

During the early years of my research work, a chance meeting with former Lostock Hall shed foreman, Barny Campbell led to a series of weekly soirees of enginemen at his residential park club house, off Wigan Road. Among the regulars were his brother, Terry, the Commons brothers, John Fletcher, Bert Stewart and Allen Green. One evening Barny suggested that, to commemorate the 25th anniversary of the shed's closure, a larger gathering of railwaymen and women from Lostock Hall and Preston should be organised.

This memorable reunion of October 1993 was probably the largest of its kind to take place in the North West, with an attendance of over 140 persons. From then on, smaller annual gatherings occurred in the Lostock Hall area, and became so popular, that the Black 5 Club, as they call themselves, now have monthly gatherings at a large pub in Preston. Here the men shunt together a train of rectangular tables end-to-end ; sit down and talk of the old days in good old Anglo-Saxon fashion. The ale runs like spring-water and the memories return amid exclamations and laughter.

The men are back again on the footplate, shovelling 'rock' and re-kindling the flames of happier times; engines emerge from the gloomy breaker's yards and once more the scalding life-blood rages, bringing men and machines together again: a physical combination of flesh, blood, iron and steam, struggling against a steep gradient with a train-load of forty-odd loose-coupled coal wagons.

The tales are spiced with a touch of irony and black humour. For instance, at a recent gathering, driver Vinny Commons and fireman, Paul Tuson were reminiscing about their part in the 1968 steam specials. Paul asked Vinny if he knew the identity of the chap who got on the footplate of their engine (45305) at Manchester. 'I don't know,' replied Vinny, 'it might have been the Devil.' Changing the subject slightly, Paul reflected on how well the engine had steamed and that she had kept a good fire in her on the day. 'Ah well, there you are,' rejoined Vinny, 'the Devil likes it hot.' I can't think of any other department on the railway, or any other industry for that matter, that continues to hold such frequent meetings so many years after closure.

Another large reunion took place in August 2008, to mark the 40th anniversary of the end of steam on B.R. This time there were men from Carnforth, Rose Grove and Lower Darwen sheds in attendance, and they all look forward to meeting up again at the big 50th.

Bob Gregson.
July 2011

Disclaimer.

Whilst every effort has been made to track down photographic sources (most of them successfully), there are one or two images which I have had in my possession for many years and for which I have no basic or adequate data to work on.

CHAPTER ONE

The Early Railway Companies

The Blackburn & Preston Railway

A line from Blackburn to Preston had been considered as early as 1840, when a consortium of local landlords and mill owners looked at the feasibility of such a venture. The idea was shelved for a while, perhaps as a result of the estimated cost of considerable engineering work in the Hoghton area. Such obstacles, however, did not detract from the enthusiasm and determination of the noted Blackburn printer and business promoter, Charles Tiplady. He regarded such a rail link with the port town of Preston as being of great benefit to the industries of Blackburn - not to mention his own share holding interests - and became the driving force behind the project. Things began to move forward quickly and in 1843 Joseph Locke was appointed engineer for the proposed line. A revised survey was carried out by his assistant, John Collister, and the bill for the Blackburn & Preston Railway (B&PR) was passed by Parliament on June 6, 1844.

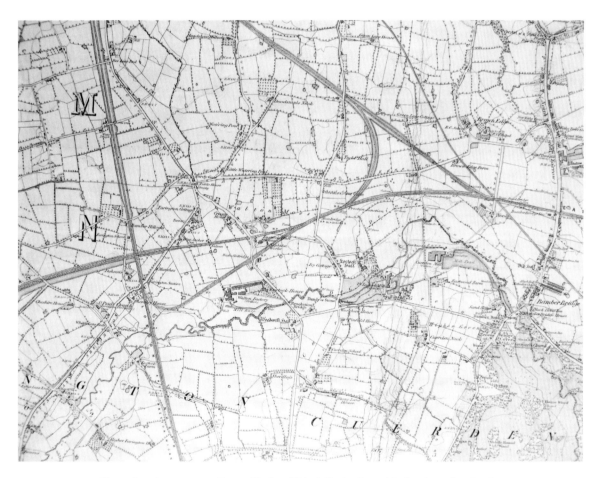

Map showing connection with the NU at Farington. *(Author's collection)*

Work commenced immediately and was carried out in two sections: Hoghton to Blackburn and Farington to Hoghton; the contractor for the former was John Stephenson and for the latter, Nowell & Hattersley. The first sod was ceremoniously cut at Hoghton on August 20, 1844 and it was the section from Hoghton to Blackburn that involved the heavier engineering work, with the line having to cross the River Darwen at Hoghton and again at Pleasington. A viaduct built of stone from the local quarry, crossed the deep and narrow gorge at Hoghton Bottoms. It has a height of 108 ft. from the river bed to the level of the track, with three arches, each having a span of 65 ft. It took eight months to build at a cost of £10,000. The following quote from a Preston journalist praises the completed work: *'Seen from the glen below, this viaduct is a truly magnificent object; blending in and not destroying the romantic grandeur of the Alpine pass, which it bestrides'*.[1] Further up the line at Pleasington, the Darwen was crossed by a timber viaduct with five spans, which carried the tracks 60 ft. above the level of the river bed. This was replaced by an imposing and more substantial stone structure in 1865.

Hoghton viaduct. *(Author's collection)*

The Farington to Hoghton section offered comparatively easy work for the engineers and navvies. The line joined the North Union (NU) railway at a point just to the south of Farington station; and from here it curved away in a westward direction to the first station on the line at Bamber Bridge. From this point the line ascended a severe 1 in 100 gradient for some three and a half miles to the east of Hoghton Station, with a short descent to Hoghton viaduct and then an ascent of around 1 in 200 for the rest of the way to Blackburn, via Pleasington and Cherry Tree stations.

Left: Blackburn & Preston Railway timetable for June 1st, 1846.
Right: Alteration of train times for January 1st, 1847.
(Both Harris Library).

The arrangement at Farington was hardly one of convenience for the B&PR. The plans drawn up from the original survey show the intended line curving to the north-west from Bamber Bridge and reaching Preston by way of a bridge over the Ribble, but this had to be abandoned when Preston Corporation objected to a third railway crossing in such close proximity to the NU and Walton Summit tramway bridges.(2) Acrimonious disputes continued between the two railway companies until the matter was finally resolved by the East Lancashire Railway in 1847. The following letter to the editor of a Preston newspaper explains what was going on at the NU end:

'Since the opening of the Blackburn and Preston Railway, there has been a deal of travelling between here and Preston, but it is an unfortunate affair that we are bound to book at the North Union Station. You have no idea of the want of every common civility, from the officers of that company to Blackburn passengers. They treat them, if I may use the term, with contempt. What reason they have I know not, and only being a raw recruit, I cannot talk technically, but it is, I hear, something about an amalgamation, or rather, the Blackburn and Preston not amalgamating with them. Now what have Blackburn and Preston passengers to do with amalgamation? The North Union are paid their toll for us to pass on their line, and I presume the demand is as much as they can for shame ask; for goodness knows their fares are high enough. There are great complaints here about this affair, and I often wonder your reporter has never mentioned it, but if you will give insertion to these few lines, if they do no good, I will trouble you again, and "walk into" a few of the North Union officers.' (3)

The line took less than two years to build at a cost of £160,000; it was inspected and passed by Captain Coddington on May 30, 1846 and opened for passengers two days later, on June 1st. The inaugural train comprised first, second and third class carriages, each painted light-blue on the lower part and black on the upper, bearing the motto: Celeritate et Utillitate, which roughly translated means 'speed and expediency'. The line was opened to goods traffic some 12 months later. Charles Tiplady was on board the first passenger train to Preston and later wrote of the occasion:

'On this day a new era in the history of Blackburn commenced by the formal opening of the Blackburn & Preston Railway line. The concourse of people witnessing the same was great and was truly gratifying to witness the splendid appearance of the line, carriages etc. I went down to Farington and was highly gratified with the trip'. (4)

Tragically, Mr Tiplady's eldest son, Charles Lomax Tiplady, was fatally injured in the railway disaster at Blackburn station in 1881.

The East Lancashire Railway

Liverpool Ormskirk & Preston section

The B&PR was amalgamated with the East Lancashire Railway (ELR) on August 3, 1846, and some two months later, the Liverpool, Ormskirk and Preston Railway (LO&PR) was absorbed into the same company. Work commenced on the LO&PR line with the time-honored cutting of the first sod at Maghull on March 16, 1847.

The company appointed Joseph Locke and John Edward Errington as engineers for the main route and a third engineer, Sturges Meek, was engaged to take charge of works in the Liverpool area. The contractors were McKenzie, Brassy & Stephenson who tendered at a cost of £200,000, with an estimated completion date of July 1, 1848. The 24 ¼ mile long route ran from Walton Junction on the Liverpool & Bury Railway to Penwortham, and connected with the Blackburn line at Lostock Hall. On completion of the line, stations were built at Midge Hall, Croston, Rufford, Burscough, Ormskirk (where a clause in the act required a branch to Skelmersdale); Aughton Park, Town Green, Maghull and Aintree.

A branch line was later opened to serve Wright & Cottam's brick works at Croston, which had a Foster's patent brick kiln capable of burning 100,000 bricks weekly. The 12 acre site also had a tram-road with steam-driven winding gear and 28 private railway wagons. Difficulties were met at Rufford, where successive attempts to build up an embankment were thwarted due to the soft, boggy ground; and with time and funds running out, a 400 yard long timber trestle had to be constructed upon piles, which had to be driven down to a depth of 40 feet before hard ground could be reached. Similar but less serious problems occurred at Croston, but more deep piling was required for a timber viaduct across the River Douglas.

The line was officially opened on Monday, April 2, 1849, following the approval of Captain Wynne R.E., a government inspector, who had passed over it the day before. There was no public celebration of the event, the unpleasant position of the company with the lessees of the North Union rendering any festive demonstration inadvisable, if indeed advisable in any circumstances.

EAST LANCASHIRE RAILWAY

MOST DIRECT AND EXPEDITIOUS ROUTE

FROM PRESTON TO SOUTHPORT,

Via East Lancashire Railway

TO ORMSKIRK

Thence per coach to Southport.

The trains leave Preston Station at 10.25 Morning, and 5.25 Evening; the whole distance being performed in one hour fifty minutes.

Fares:- First Class, 5s.; Second Class and inside Coach, 4s. 6d.; Second Class and outside Coach, 3s. 6d.; Third Class, 3s.

The coach leaves the Scarisbrick Arms Hotel, Southport, for Ormskirk and Preston at 9.15 Morning and 4.15 Evening.

R. HACKING.

General Manager's Office, Bury, 16th April 1849.

Preston Chronicle, April 21st 1849

Midge Hall station & the spacious goods yard with shed in the background. *(BRB Residuals. Leyland Library)*

The on-going feud between the two companies sparked off a competition in ticket prices: On Thursday last, the fares were only sixpence each, third class to Liverpool; ninepence second class and one shilling first. On Thursday night, the NU people tired of this game and raised their fares to one shilling and sixpence, two shillings and sixpence and three shillings and sixpence. The ELR yet takes passengers at one shilling, one shilling and sixpence and two shillings. The reduction of fares naturally caused great numbers of persons to travel to Liverpool yesterday. [5]

For many years the 4.40 pm. Liverpool Exchange to Blackpool and Skipton stopped at Midge Hall, where the rear Skipton portion, comprising old non-corridor stock, was detached. With the Blackpool train out of the way, a Lostock Hall engine, which had been waiting in the goods loop, coupled-up to the rear portion and took the train on to Skipton, by way of Blackburn and the Great Harwood -

Padiham loop. It has been noted that this 64 mile route must have been one of the longest trips in the country using non-corridor vehicles.

Advertisement from Preston Guardian August 10th 1878.

The Bamber Bridge and Preston extension

Trains from Liverpool had to reverse from Lostock Hall to get to Preston and it was this factor, together with the high tolls exacted for use of the Farington - Preston section that prompted the ELR to apply again for an independent route into Preston. Notwithstanding strong opposition from the NU and Preston Corporation, the bill was passed on July 22, 1847; the Corporation managing to secure a clause in the act which obliged the ELR to create an ornamental park at the north end of the Ribble viaduct, with walkways, flower beds, shrubberies and water features. This was well planned out and merged beautifully with the existing park at Avenham.

Advertisement from the Preston Guardian, September 7th 1850.

Preston Chronicle, November 16th 1850

Work on the 'Bamber Bridge and Preston Extension' as it became known, began in November 1848, with the main contractors, McCormick & Daglish, sub-contracting the work to Bridgewater & Crowther. The biggest obstacle involved the crossing of the flood plain between Whitehouse and the Ribble, where the ground was deemed to be too soft to take an earth and gravel embankment.

A viaduct was therefore constructed, comprising 52 brick arches, each with a span of 30ft., and deep pile-driving was required for each pier before solid ground could be reached. On Thursday, October 25, 1849, the work was set back by several months, following the collapse of 13 arches during a period of particularly bad weather. Fifteen of the arches had already been completed before the disaster occurred and six others were in progress. Most of the piers had been completed and were ready to receive their arches. The arches complete or in the course of completion were those from the 17th to the 37th (numbered from the Ribble bridge). The timber centering of arches 37 to 26 had been slackened off for some time, but that of arch No. 27 had only been slackened on the previous Tuesday. The centering of arch No. 16 and those between Nos. 27 and 37 remained in situ. The piers were built upon timber pile foundations, with timber sheeting some eight or nine inches thick fixed to the sides.

The soil in this part of the valley was of a mossy, spongy nature (bog soil), and the piles would needed to have been driven down into firmer ground which, apparently, was not the case with some of them. The combined weight of each arch and one pier is around 120 tons, there being some 81 yards of brickwork in each. Arches Nos. 17 to 21 were given a membrane of asphalt, this being a composition of pitch, sand and gravel; the purpose being to prevent the ingress of rain and to enable the mortar to set; in the long term it also protected the brickwork. At the time of the accident, the other arches had not been asphalted. It had been raining for some days, causing flooding in the adjoining fields and washing away the mortar in places. The masonry collapsed shortly after one o 'clock on Thursday afternoon. Such was the condition of the weather at the time that only a few workmen were in the vicinity of the construction site and there were no injuries. The remarkable thing about it was that only the day before, over 100 workmen were employed upon and around the arches.

Arch No. 27, is alleged to have been the first one to give way, and this appears to be probable, as an inspection of the remaining piers on each side of the arch, found them to have vertical cracks in the brickwork and leaning slightly over towards each other, indicating great pressure from the adjoining masonry. The two arches from which the centering had not been slackened, Nos. 28 and 29, and the ten arches on the other side of No. 27, fell almost immediately together, No. 17 being the last to give way. Arch No. 16 would in all probability have given way as well, but for the fact that the pier between it and No. 17 was almost three times the thickness of the others and consequently able to stand the pressure upon it. Together with the thirteen arches, the pier between Nos. 24 and 25 collapsed completely, and most of the surviving piers were so badly damaged they had to be taken down and rebuilt. Soon after the accident occurred, the sub-contractors along with two works inspectors attended the scene. A number of men were quickly appointed to prevent the arches nearest the Penwortham reservoir from going the same way as the others. Large timber beams and planks were procured and they set about shoring-up the piers either side of arch No. 30. The senior inspector of works, Mr Mason (appropriate name), on having surveyed the remaining parts of the viaduct concluded that:

'The 18th pier from the river is, we perceive from an inspection of the ruins, slightly cracked at the bottom. A portion of the brickwork above the stone springers of the 19th is left standing to a considerable height, and the lower portion of the pier has sustained a considerable crack. The 20th, 21st and 22nd piers are also cracked at the bottom, and the 23rd is cracked in the centre of the brickwork and at the bottom as well, a large portion of the work above the springers remaining. The 24th pier leans considerably towards the Penwortham reservoir and has sustained a large crack at the bottom. The 25th is entirely down, the brick and stonework being distributed with the brickwork of the arches on each side of it. The 26th is also cracked and the 27th is only injured, a thick piece of timber between it and the 28th having been split by the pressure. The 29th leans towards the Ribble and has sustained several large cracks, and the pier on the other side leans the other way'. [6]

Postcard showing Ribble bridge & viaduct *(Author's collection)*

A disturbing account given by the Preston Guardian would have been enough to discourage the hardiest traveller from crossing the viaduct on a train:

'There have been various rumours afloat as to the cause of the accident, some attributing it to the rain having softened the mortar and preventing it setting; others to the badness of the materials, the mortar being stated to contain very little lime and too much sand, mixed with a quantity of common soil; and others to the bad workmanship throughout. We have been given to understand that representations have frequently been made to the contractors that the arches would never stand, but must give way

the first time a train passed over them, if not before. Some time ago, in a case where the contractors were summoned by several of the workmen for non-payment of wages, it was strongly rumoured that disclosures would be made by the plaintiffs respecting the badness of the workmanship of the arches; but such disclosures, however, were not made. The contractors will suffer a heavy loss from the accident; and, in addition, the opening of this track of the East Lancashire Railway Company's line will be delayed for a considerable period. Providentially, no person was injured by the accident; had it been otherwise there would no doubt have been a searching investigation into its cause, and the whole of the circumstances connected with the erection of the arches.' [7]

Engineers Errington and Meek, however, had every confidence in the structure and to prove it they travelled across both the viaduct and Ribble bridge with a 'test train' on August 15, 1850. The train consisted of two of the company's heaviest locomotives and a considerable number of open wagons laden with earth. After several such crossings, the masonry was examined and found to be satisfactory. The viaduct began to show signs of subsidence some years after the line was opened (this was probably due to heavier axle-loads) and many of the piers and arches had to be braced with iron tie-bars and flanges.

The undulating structure was eventually converted to an embankment in 1883, at a considerable cost to the new owners, the Lancashire & Yorkshire Railway (LYR); they had indeed inherited a nightmare. The masonry itself remained in situ and was filled in for the most part with mining slag, hard clay rubble and rubbish from local tips, all blinded with layers of sand, cinders and gravel. It is rumoured that some of the infill came from the excavations at Lostock Hall engine shed site.

The Ribble bridge was a magnificent structure and a worthy complement to Charles Vignoles' five-arched masterpiece in stone, further downstream. It comprised four stone piers with brick panels carrying three 100 ft. arched iron spans over the river; these were of the segmented iron pattern with open spandrels, cornice and blocking, which gave a total weight of just over 500 tons. The ironwork was supervised by Mr. John Harrison, who was the agent for Messrs. Butler & Co. of Stannington, near Leeds, the work being completed on January 27, 1850. The piers on either bank had a thickness of 15 ft. 6 ins. and incorporated semicircular brick arches, each having a span of 25 ft. and trimmed with stone quoins, voussoirs and copings.

The Ribble Bridge as seen from the Broad Walk in Miller Park *(Harris Museum)* and the '40 steps' on the north bank, which give access to the bridge from Avenham Park. *(Harris Library)*

One of the terms of agreement laid down by the Corporation was that provision be made for a public right of way across the river; the viaduct was therefore fitted with cantilever brackets on the east side, upon which a narrow footpath was constructed. Access to the path on the north bank was by way of a steep flight of 40 stone steps, which followed the wing wall at 90 degrees to the bridge; and the south end was accessed by another flight of stone steps, keyed-in to the bridge masonry at the top and facing south, with halfway landing supported on a brick pier. It was later reversed at the landing into a 'dog-leg' pattern when the viaduct was filled in. The iron spans were replaced with an ugly steel girder and plate structure by the London Midland and Scottish (LMS) railway in 1930.

A fine Victorian view of the bridge from Miller Park. LYR radial tank hauling a train of non-corridor stock for either Blackburn or Liverpool, with a 'birdcage' brake at the front. *(Harris Museum)*

Miller Park on a typical Sunday afternoon or bank holiday in Edwardian days. LYR 4-4-0 express locomotive crosses the bridge with a six coach train for Blackpool *(Harris Museum)*

Aerial Photo showing the original Ribble bridge and East Lancs station and yard. July. 1925. (*British Railways*)

20

North of the Ribble crossing, the line was carried on a landscaped embankment traversing an area formally known as Wyse's Gardens, which ended at the last over-bridge before Preston. The Town Clerk required this structure to be so designed as to harmonise with the graceful surroundings, and the finished work must have gone beyond his greatest expectations.

'Ivy Bridge', as it later became known to Prestonians, owing to a profusion of this araliaceous evergreen obscuring much of the masonry on the west side, was constructed of coursed ashlar stone with rusticated joints and rock faced voussoirs. Because of the limited height it has an elliptical arch and crosses the Broad Walk between the Avenham and Miller Parks on a 30 ft. skew over to the south-west, 12 ft. from the square. The parapets comprise bulbous cast iron balusters with stone copings, and alternate stone panels; there being four sets of four balusters on each parapet, with a half baluster at the end of each stone panel and parapet end.

A set of decorative wrought iron gates, located midway beneath the arch, completed what can only be described as a work of art. In 1874 the bridge was widened on the East side, to allow for a third track in the form of a long shunting siding, which terminated a short distance from the Ribble viaduct. The line entered the yard at Preston by way of a short cutting above which a bridge was built to connect East Cliff with the town.

The driver of 0-4-4 tank, No.43, poses for the cameraman on the ornamental Ivy Bridge
between shunting duties, circa 1900. *(Authors Collection)*

Vicar's Bridge, as it became known, was named after the vicarage nearby, which was the residence of the Rev J.O. Parr, vicar of Saint George's Church, off Lune Street. Other properties on the Cliff at that time, were occupied by the Rev. J. Clay, Mr. E. Harrison and Alderman German respectively. The bridge is a single span lattice girder type and was constructed by Mr Daglish's company from components fabricated at his workshops in St. Helen's, in accordance with Mr Fairbourn's patent.

The finished work measured 140 ft. in length by 28 ft. 6 ins. in width, with a height of 25 ft. from the track bed to the underside of the girders. The box parapets are 9 ft. 6 ins. high by 18 ins. wide and are made up of inner and outer lattice work, comprising 3½ ins. x ¼ ins. wrought-iron flat strip, riveted at the intersections, with horizontal and vertical bracing and riveted iron plates top and bottom. The underside has 15 transverse H-section riveted iron girders, upon which timber planking was laid lengthwise. This form of decking became unsuitable for heavier traffic, and was replaced in 1971 by a single-track bailey type structure with cantilever footbridge. The work was carried out by the Royal Engineers and was intended to be a temporary facility only, but when the R.E. get involved, the completed work is invariably of such good quality as to last for many years which, indeed, has been the case with this particular bridge. The Bailey is secured by tensioned anchors on each abutment, and although it is located within the framework of the old structure, it is entirely independent of it. Such is the condition of Vicar's Bridge at the time of writing, that it will soon be unable to carry its own weight and will have to be removed. The bailey will remain in situ until plans are drawn-up for a new bridge.

The south-east approach wall for the road comprises ashlar stone and measures 28 ft. 9½ ins. in length by 6ft from the road surface to the top of the coping stones and has a width of 27 ins. There is a large capping stone at the east end, 7 ft. 2 ins. by 19 ins.; the smaller coping stones have a height of 8 ins. The north-west wall is 46 ft. 9 ins. long and the south-west wall has a length of 29 ft., curving round from east to south. Both walls have the same characteristics as the south-east one, and the north-east wall was removed some time ago to accommodate a stairway to the car park below. It had been the original intention of the company to erect a three-arched brick bridge on the site, but such a structure would have seriously restricted the number of tracks entering the station and yard area.

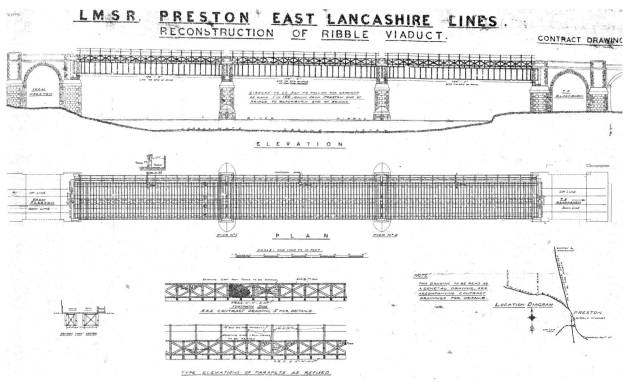

Contract drawing for the replacement steelwork on the Ribble bridge.
Note the gradient of 1 in 100 from the Preston end *(Mike Norris)*

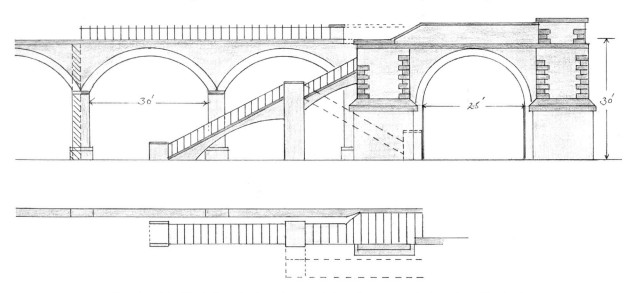

Drawing No D301. Plan & elevation of stairs at south end of bridge *(Author)*

Fairburn 2-6-4 tank, 42154, crosses the Ribble bridge
with a local train for Southport in the 1960's. *(Stan Withers)*

Lostock Hall Stanier 2-6-4 tank, 42436, approaches the Ribble bridge with a local passenger train
for Southport in the 1950's *(Jack Hodgkinson)*

The NU enlarged its station at Preston to accommodate ELR traffic and allocated an entrance to them on Butler Street. The original plan was to by-pass the NU station and join up with the Lancaster and Preston Railway to the north of the town at Dock Street, but this was turned down by the House of Lords in 1847, and they were compelled to have recourse to the NU station. It was opened for passenger traffic on September 2, 1850 and for goods some two months later. The NU insisted on both parts of the station being operated by its own staff and management and all costs shared by both companies; this stipulation naturally led to arguments over costs, responsibilities and liabilities, and arbitrators were frequently called in. After years of haggling, the issues were finally settled in 1856 by a remarkable man of many talents, Mr. Isambard Kingdom Brunel.

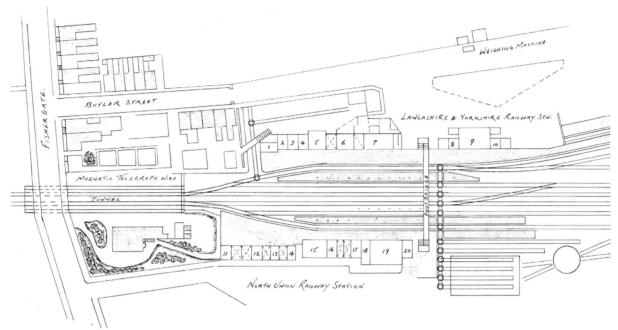

Preston Station in the 1850's, showing tunnel at Fishergate.

Key to numbers:

E.L.R. side: (1) Wash rooms; (2) Waiting rooms; (3) Magnetic telegraph office; (4) Station Master's office; (5) Booking office; (6) Waiting room; (7) Refreshment rooms; (8) Waiting room; (9) Parcels office); (10) Waiting room.

N.U. side: (11) Lamp room; (12) left luggage office; (13) Inspector's office; (14) Electric Telegraph office; (15) Waiting room; (16) Booking office; (17) Parcel office; (18) Waiting room; (19) Refreshment room); (20) Wash rooms.

Most of the hostilities were perpetrated by the NU who resented the ELR , regarding them as potential rivals and the proximity of their operations as both intrusive and obstructive. They did their best to make things as difficult as possible for those wishing to use the EL services; and the following examples serve to illustrate the extent to which they were prepared to go.

Mr. Thomas Barker, a Preston coal merchant and regular user of both railway companies, wished to travel to Blackburn one day. He went into the booking office, but was unable to obtain a ticket. He then went to see Mr. Byrne, the superintendent, but he refused to take money and issue a ticket, so Mr Barker returned to the ticket window for another try and found a wedding party there, similarly circumstanced with himself. He returned to the platform and, after remonstrating with Mr. Byrne, he was referred to the guard, who arranged for them to go by the train and pay at Blackburn. On speaking to Mr. Entwistle, the superintendent at Blackburn, he was told that the annoyance was of a 'daily occurrence'.

Mr. James Woods had a similar experience when desiring to purchase a ticket to Liverpool. The ticket clerk turned his back on him and proceeded to look through the pigeon-holes for some two and a half minutes. Mr. Woods repeated his request and this was followed by a further delay of 3 to 4 minutes. On his third attempt, the clerk turned round to face him and stated that the train was 'off.' Not only were these official prevarications costing travellers their valuable time, they were also costing them unnecessary expenditure: Mr. Josiah Goodwin Kershaw, a stockbroker from Leeds, arrived at the station at 6.30 pm. and asked for a ticket to Manchester. He was informed by the clerk that there were no more trains to Manchester that evening, so Mr. Kershaw had to book into a hotel for the night.

An unidentifiable Super D crossing the Ribble bridge with a train of coal empties
for Bamber Bridge in the 1950's *(Jack Hodgkinson)*

On his return to the station the following morning, he discovered that he could have travelled to Manchester the evening before by a 7 pm. train. He complained to one of the EL directors, who explained the situation and added that it was a 'frequent occurrence'. The ELR goods traffic suffered in much the same way, and such was the extent of the deliberately planned delays, that the company had to cart goods by road some three miles to Bamber Bridge.

Mr. Samuel Smith, a general merchant of Preston, and a regular client of the ELR, had to do likewise and then load the goods onto a train at Bamber Bridge for the remainder of the journey to Manchester. He had little faith in the authorities at Preston station, and as far as he was concerned, the EL goods service was 'useless.' He had been under the impression that the ELR carted their goods in order to avoid pontage tolls on the Ribble bridge (which had never been levied). As a regular visitor to Preston station, he saw for himself the state of affairs, which he described as 'presenting a scene of great confusion' and witnessed the frequent complaints relating to the protracted detainment of goods at the station.

Following the amalgamation of the ELR with the LYR in 1859, relations with the NU improved slightly; and all ostentatious and tangible animosities disappeared once the new station was up and running in 1880. There was greater co-operation and more effective organisation between the two companies, which made things a lot easier for management, staff, agents and the public alike; moreover, with the establishment of the Railway Benevolent Institution in 1858 [8]; and the ASLEF union (Associated Society of Locomotive Engineers and Firemen) in 1880; and the founding of the Preston Railway Servant's Sick and Burial Society in 1881 [9], the servants of both companies shared a mutual interest in the various aspects of their employment, and a solidarity regarding their rights, entitlements, hours of duty and pay etc. This was emphasised on Sunday, March 8, 1880, when over 150 men from both companies assembled on the main island platform at 2.30 pm. and proceeded to Christ Church, to hear the Rev. Frith give a special sermon for LYR fireman, Robert Clarkson, who was killed in the Burscough Junction collision in January that year. A total of £30.00 was raised on behalf of his widow and five young children. [10]

Further Junctions & Connections

The Bamber Bridge & Preston Extension was connected to the Liverpool line in 1850, by means of a continuous south-west/north-west curve from Lostock Hall to a junction less than a mile to the north-west of Bamber Bridge. Two years later, a small station was built in the fork and was given the name, Preston Junction. [11] From that time onward, the connecting curve to Lostock Hall was always known as the Preston Junction Fork.

Passengers had to cross the line to reach the station, and this resulted in the death of at least one person, which brought forth calls for the erection of a bridge, and a right of way from Brownedge to Toad Lane (later changed to Todd Lane). The LYR also received complaints regarding the inadequate height of the platforms and how elderly folks and ladies with children had to struggle when getting in and out of trains. Tenders were subsequently invited for the construction of a footbridge and raising of the platforms in 1884, but the plans were discarded following a decision to build a new station with island platform on the north side of 'Toad Lane' bridge in 1885.

Preston Chronicle, February 9th 1884

LANCASHIRE AND YORKSHIRE RAILWAY

The Directors are prepared to receive TENDERS for the erection of a footbridge and raising of platforms at Preston Junction Station. Plans and Specifications may be seen, and quantities with forms of tender obtained at the Engineer's Offices. Manchester, on and after Monday, the 11th inst. Tenders endorsed " Tenders for Footbridge and raising of Platforms at Preston Junction Station", and addressed to the Directors, to be in the hands of the undersigned not later than 10 o'clock on Monday morning, the 18th February.

J.H. STAFFORD, Secretary.

Manchester, 8th February, 1884.

The down platform of the original station was retained and 'looped' for the inspection of tickets on trains with non-corridor stock. Over the decades, the name Preston Junction was the cause of much confusion to those who were strangers to the area and travelling to the main station in Preston. The name, however, survived until 1952 when British Railways changed it to Todd Lane Junction.

On May 3, 1886, another junction was opened at Farington, connecting the former B&PR line to the NU to allow south-bound trains from East Lancashire to by-pass Preston. The 'Back Line', as it was referred to by generations of Lostock Hall men, however, saw very little in the way of passenger service and was used mainly for goods and diversion purposes.

The journey time from Liverpool to Preston was shortened with the opening on July 1, 1891 of a connecting line from a junction near Moss Lane to a junction with the NU at Penwortham, to the north of Farington Station. This enabled trains from Liverpool to reach Preston without having to negotiate the Preston Junction Curve, thus reducing the journey time to 35 minutes; the only draw-back being that trains would have to use the NU platforms at Preston. This particular route, however, was to be used by express trains only with connections at Preston for northern and Scottish traffic; local stopping services would continue to use the Preston Junction curve.

The line left the NU at Farington Curve Junction taking a south-westerly course on a fairly steep gradient for about a quarter of a mile; it then levelled out up to a point close to the church at Farington and then climbed again up to Moss Lane Junction. The contractors were Etheridge & Clarke, of Manchester and this comparatively short stretch of line took the best part of two years to build. The problems began when hard clay was encountered, being further hampered by long periods of heavy rainfall. The engineers had planned to slope the sides of the cutting from the level of the permanent way, but large quantities of earth began to break away and slide down. Costs and time increased as thick retaining walls with deep foundations had to be put in place. Two girder bridges on brick piers were included in the contract.

On May 25, 1908, the LYR opened a connection between Lostock Hall and the Liverpool line at Farington Curve, enabling trains from East Lancashire to join the main line and run into the west side of Preston Station. This was a particularly steep section, where goods trains had to stop to allow the guard to pin down wagon brakes before descending.

By using the curve at Preston Junction it was now possible to move freight between the east and west goods yards at Preston, without getting in the way of main line traffic to the north of the station. It also came in useful for trains from the north of Preston bound for Blackpool and Fleetwood; they could now make the journey without having to stop at Preston for the engine to run round the train and use the turntable at the shed. Finally, following a meeting between a deputation from Preston Council and some of the directors of the LYR at Manchester on Wednesday, October 26, 1864, the ownership of the old Preston & Walton Summit tram road was transferred to the Corporation of Preston:

'It is considered certain that before long, the tramway, which has for years been considered "an antiquated nuisance", will be handed over to the Corporation, who will make it into a public walkway and plant it on each side, as far as Penwortham, with trees etc.' [12]

FOOTNOTES

[1] Preston Guardian, June 6th 1846.

[2] (a) The tram bridge carried the first railway as such across the Ribble at Preston in 1803, linking the Lancaster Canal to the Leeds & Liverpool Canal via Walton Summit. It had 7 spans, two of 45 ft. 2 ins.; two of 44 ft.; one of 44 ft. 6 ins.; one of 43 ft.; and one of 42 ft. 6 ins. It had an average headway in the centre of 15ft. 9 ins. above average high-water, ordinary spring tides.
(b) The North Union bridge was completed in 1839. It was built of rusticated ashlar stone from quarries at Lancaster, Whittle and Longridge, and comprised five elliptical arches, each having a span of 120 ft. Brick relieving arches are located in the spaces between the main arches, in order to diminish the super-incumbent pressure and divert the weight upon the piers; the versed-sine of each arch being 33 ft.
 The foundation stone was laid by Mr. W.M. Taylor, one of the company's directors, on 1st September, 1835. The contract was awarded to Henry Mullins and McMahon, Bridge Masons of Dublin, and the cost of construction was £40,000. The total length is 872 ft. with an original width of 28 ft. The abutments are 30ft. thick and the wing walls are 67 ft. in length, each being built upon piles some 11 to 16 ft. in depth.
The height from the river bed to the top of the parapet is 68 ft. and the high-water mark to the keystone of each arch is 50 ft. The bridge was widened to double its original width in 1879, and a box-girder and lattice bridge was added to the west side in 1904. This, together with the electrification gantries, has considerably detracted the former elegance of this imposing structure.

[3] Preston Chronicle, Saturday 15, August, 1846.

[4] Blackburn Museum.

[5] Preston Guardian, April 7, 1849.

[6] Preston Guardian, October 27, 1849.

[7] ibid.

[8] The first meeting of the RBI was held at Crewe on May 8, 1858, with Joseph Locke M.P. as chairman.

[9] The Preston Railway Servant's Sick and Burial Society was established on Sunday, October 2nd 1881, when a procession of some 200 men from both companies, left the main island platform to attend a service at the Parish Church at 2 pm. A collection was then subscribed to the Preston and County of Lancaster Royal Infirmary. (Preston Guardian, October 8, 1881)

[10] Among those present were Mr. Miles, station master (LNW) and his assistant, Mr. Lomax; and Mr. Nield, station master (LYR). It was this overwhelming charitable response that led to the founding of the Preston Railway Servant's Sick and Burial Society.
The collection was not confined to the railway itself; a further sum of £55. 7s was raised by the town's business community. (Preston Guardian, February 14, 1880)

[11] Prior to this, the south-west end of the curve was known as Preston Junction.

[12] The deputation comprised Alderman Miller, Alderman Parker and Councilor Park, accompanied by the Town Clerk and the Borough Steward. (Preston Guardian, October 29, 1864)

CHAPTER TWO

The West Lancashire Railway

An Interesting Aerial view of the West Lancs river bridge with the Fishergate terminus and yard at the top right. This picture was taken for the LYR in 1920. Note the amount of passenger stock. *(British Railways)*

It was possible to travel from Preston to Southport by train in 1856 via Burscough Junction on the former LO&PR. A more direct route was envisaged and planned by the West Lancashire Railway (WLR), and a bill was passed on August 17, 1871. The Company appointed Mr C.D. Fox as engineer and the contractors were Clarke, Punshard & Company. The first sod was cut at Southport on April 18, 1873 by the Lord Mayor of the town, Alderman Samuel Swire. From an engineering point of view the work from Hesketh Park to Hesketh Bank presented no major difficulties. There were, however, considerable financial difficulties which hindered progress from the outset and were to continue throughout the company's brief existence. The line to Hesketh Bank was belatedly opened to passenger traffic on February 19, 1878, with intermediate stations at Churchtown, Crossens, Banks and Hundred End.

A short branch line was constructed from Hesketh Bank to wharves on the Rufford branch of the Leeds & Liverpool Canal at Tarleton. It was opened to passenger traffic on June 3, 1912, and the service was operated by a steam-powered rail motor which ran from Crossens via Hesketh Bank. An unstaffed halt called Boatyard Crossing was opened halfway between Hesketh Bank and Tarleton, but the branch was poorly patronised by local people and the service was withdrawn on October 1, 1913. It continued to be used for goods until its complete closure by the LMS railway in November 1930. A swing bridge over the River Douglas was necessary in order to facilitate the passage of steam boats and involved some major engineering work, as the river had to be widened and deepened at this point.

Deep piling was required, and a total of 24 cylindrical iron piles had to be driven down to a depth of 20 ft. and filled-in with some 4000 cubic yards of ferro-concrete before the piers could be built. Each pier, where exposed to the river, had to be guarded by a protective wall of timber piling as a precaution against ramming by vessels or heavy objects borne down the river during times of flooding.

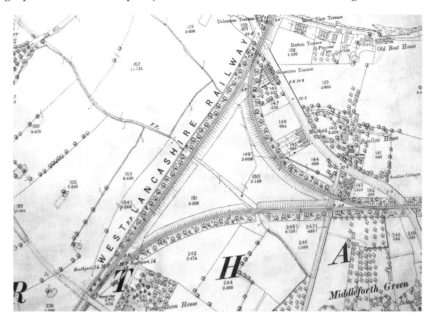

1896 Map showing Penwortham triangle *(Harris Library)*

Further problems in the form of hard clay were encountered in various places, from the banks of the Douglas to the south bank of the Ribble at Penwortham; this made the excavation work twice as laborious and the contract began to fall further behind. The problem was solved when the engineer took delivery of one of the new steam shovels, which was quite possibly the first of its kind to be used on railway construction in the North West.

This revolutionary machine was put to use immediately and the remainder of the line to Penwortham was completed with comparative ease. Originally, only two stations, Hoole and Longton, were built between Hesketh Bank and the Ribble bridge. Later, in 1889, a station was built at Howick, and another at Penwortham called Cop Lane was opened in 1911. To complicate matters, Longton was re-named Longton Bridge in 1892 and Howick was changed to Hutton & Howick in 1898, only to be changed again to New Longton & Hutton in 1924. Ambiguity at Cop Lane was dispelled in 1940, when the LMS changed the name to Penwortham Cop Lane.

WLR Station, Back Elevation *(Drawings by Author, from WLR Plans courtesy of Mike Norris)*

WLR Station, Side Elevation

WLR Station, Front Elevation

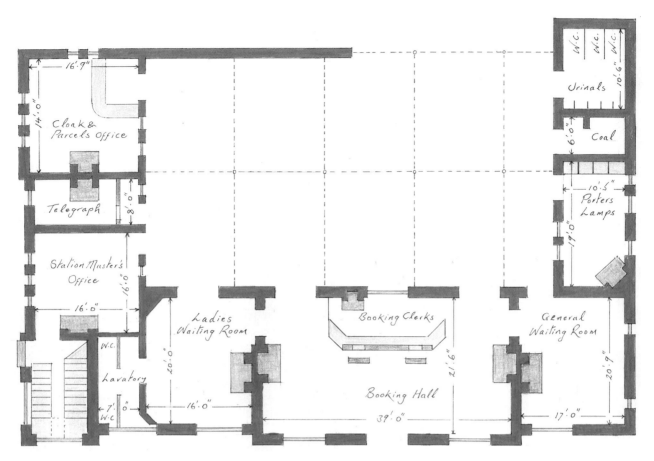

WLR Station, Ground Floor Plan

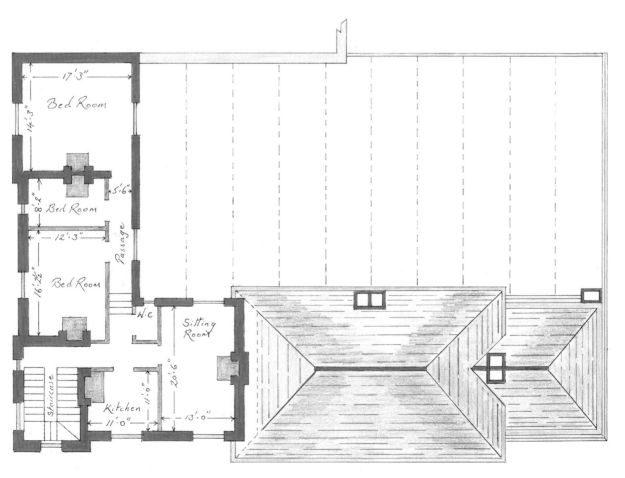

WLR First Floor plan

31

The Ribble crossing at Penwortham involved a lot of major preparatory work before the bridge could be built; and for reasons associated with future navigation plans, Preston Corporation stipulated an 80 ft. wide excavation, taken down to a depth of 10 ft. into the sandstone rock, for the full width of the river. This added considerably to the construction costs and completion time, which was further set back for a period of some weeks when the river flooded on Sunday, July 31, 1881. This was due to a combination of a series of heavy downpours and a high tide, which caused the Ribble to rise 8 ft. above its normal high-water level. The corner of one of the coffer-dams close to the middle of the stream gave way and the water rushed in with great force, carrying away wheelbarrows, large blocks of timber and some of the workmen's equipment. Fortunately nobody was working there that day. Much the same thing occurred again on Wednesday, August 10, but preparations had been made this time, and nothing was lost. [1]

The bridge comprised six piers made of stone from Longridge quarries (one on each bank and four in the river) and five iron spans of lengths varying from 58 ft. to 60 ft. (see drawing details). The ironwork for all the bridges on this line was supplied and fixed by the Stockton Forge and the work was supervised by their resident engineer, Mr Blackburn. At the south-west end there were iron bridges spanning Leyland and Riverside Roads. The line approached the bridge in a north easterly direction and began a gentle northward curve from the fourth pier to the end of the bridge. From this point it continued to curve over to the north-west across another iron bridge, over Broadgate and a masonry viaduct of twelve arches, before entering the goods yard and terminus at Fishergate Hill. The Leyland Road bridge was provided with additional support on the south side in the form of two girder stanchions, located approximately 10 ft. from the stone abutment on the road side of the kerb; these, together with the longer, horizontal bridge girders and plates, were moved into position by a local man with a traction engine, Mr. William Grime, of Broadgate. [2]

The newly completed Ribble bridge, photographed in the 1880's from the north bank.
Ribble Junction box can be seen beyond the Leyland Road bridge. *(Harris Museum)*

Work in progress on the pipeline over Broadgate (Jim Heron archive)

Fitting gas main on Ribble bridge: a LNW loco is in attendance as the steam crane prepares to move a section of gas pipe from the bridge onto the steel ducting *(Jim Heron archive)*

Looking from the north end. Note the slow curve of the structure and the gradient post on the right, indicating a fall of 1 in 100 towards Preston. *(Jim Heron archive)*.

The sixteen mile line from Southport to Preston was finally completed after nine and a half years, and on Friday, September 1, the line was thoroughly inspected by General Hutchinson, the Board of Trade Inspector. The first trial run over the Ribble bridge was made early that morning with a heavy locomotive and a train comprising first, second and third class carriages, carrying, among others, Mr. C. D. Fox and another railway engineer, Mr. James Brunlees (who had been invited to the occasion by the company); Mr. Thursby, the company's resident engineer; Messrs. Braddock and Matthews (the contractors responsible for completing the line) and Mr Gilbert, the WLR manager.

WEST LANCASHIRE RAILWAY.

THE DIRECT ROUTE TO SOUTHPORT.

SPECIAL NOTICE.

On and after January Next, the Company will issue **THIRD CLASS CONTRACT TICKETS**, between **SOUTHPORT** and **PRESTON**, as under, viz. :-

12 Months	6 Months	3 Months
£11 4s. 0d.	£5 12s. 0d.	£3 12s. 0d.

With Five per cent for Government Duty.

Terms of Application can be obtained at any Station, or from the General Offices of the Company, Central Station, Southport - By order,
                                                                                Thomas Gilbert, General
Manager.
Southport, 6th December, 1882.

Preston Guardian, December 9th 1882

Preston Guardian, December 23ʳᵈ 1882

Later on, the Ribble bridge was tested again, this time with a heavier load consisting of four engines which stood on the bridge for some time and then ran back and forth several times at various speeds. The deflection was recorded at a quarter of an inch, [3] which was regarded as quite satisfactory, and the whole line was deemed fit for service by the General. The grand opening ceremony took place on Tuesday, September 5, 1882, with a lengthy train from Southport to Preston; and on their arrival at Fishergate, the guests were not to be deterred by the fact that the terminus building (as with the one at Southport) was still under construction; indeed, many of them were keen to see the work in progress. Both terminus buildings were designed by the noted London railway architect, Charles Driver. They were of the Gothic style and well laid out with the usual facilities on the ground floor and an apartment for the station master and his family on the first floor (see drawings). The line was officially opened for normal traffic on the following Monday, September 11, in good time for the Preston Guild Merchant. [4]

The station had a 400 ft. long island platform which was partly protected from the elements by a 210 ft. long open-sided canopy, comprising eight glazed, transverse gables, supported by three rows of eight cast-iron columns. The goods yard to the west of the station was opened for traffic on February 15, 1883, having two low-level sidings, a coal yard and substantial goods shed. The station signal box, a McKenzie and Holland design with 30 levers, was opened on the same day. Later on, a small two-road engine shed was built, complete with coaling stage, water tank and turntable. The price of a return ticket to Southport in that year was one shilling, and half fare for those under the age of 13.

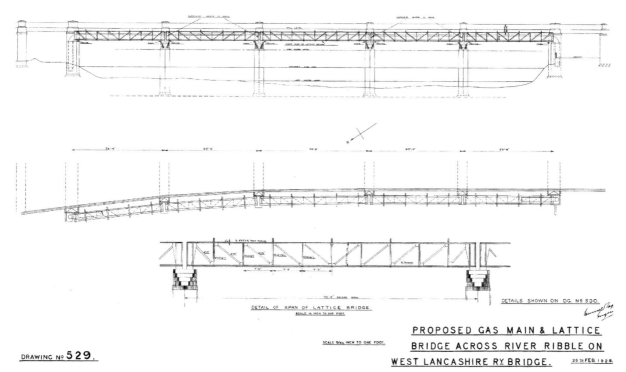

DRAWING Nº **529**.

DETAIL OF SPAN OF LATTICE BRIDGE.

DETAILS SHOWN ON DG. Nº 530.

**PROPOSED GAS MAIN & LATTICE
BRIDGE ACROSS RIVER RIBBLE ON
WEST LANCASHIRE RY BRIDGE.** 25ᵗʰ FEB 1928

Contract drawings for the Preston gas Company (NW Gas) showing pipe and
ducting detail on the WL bridge (National Grid Archive)

For 1st October 1896 until further notice (Weekdays):			
Time (Arr.)	Time (Dep).	From	Destination
7.21 a.m.		6.40 a.m. Southport Central	Preston W.L.
8.37 a.m.	8.48 a.m.	7.55 a.m. Southport Central	Blackburn
9.33 a.m.		7.00 a.m. Liverpool Central	Preston W.L.
10.42 a.m.		10.00 a.m. Southport Central	Preston W.L.
12.22 p.m.	12.30 p.m.	11.40 a.m. Southport Central	Blackburn
1.42 p.m.		1.00 p.m. Southport Central	Preston W.L.
3.17 p.m.		2.35 p.m. Southport Central	Preston W.L.

For 1st October 1896 until further notice (Weekdays):			
Time (Arr.)	Time (Dep).	From	Destination
	6.15 a.m.	6.15 a.m. Preston W.L.	Liverpool Central
	7.55 a.m.	7.55 a.m. Preston W.L.	Southport Central
	8.50 a.m.	8.50 a.m. Preston W.L.	Southport Central
9.58 a.m.	10.10 a.m.	9.30 a.m. Blackburn	Southport Central
	11.35 a.m.	11.35 a.m. Preston W.L.	Liverpool Central
	12.1 p.m.	12.1 p.m. Preston W.L.	Southport Central
	1.15 p.m.	1.15 p.m. Preston W.L.	Southport Central
2.8 p.m.	2.15 p.m.	1.40 p.m. Blackburn	Southport Central
	4.0 p.m.	4.0 p.m. Preston W.L.	Southport Central
	4.45 p.m. **SX**	4.45 p.m. Preston W.L.	Southport Central
5.24 p.m.	5.32 p.m.	5.5 p.m. Blackburn	Southport Central
	6.20 p.m.	6.20 p.m. Preston W.L.	Southport Central
	7.5 p.m.	7.5 p.m. Preston W.L.	Liverpool Central
	8.10 p.m.	8.10 p.m. Preston W.L.	Longton Bridge
	9.15 p.m. **SO**	9.15 p.m. Preston W.L.	Barton
9.23 p.m. **SX**	9.30 p.m. **SX**	8.55 p.m. Blackburn	Southport Central
9.58 p.m. **SO**	10.30 p.m. **SO**	9.20 p.m. Blackburn	Southport Central

Southport Central was the WLR terminus adjacent to LYR. Southport Chapel St. station.

A 2-6-4 tank with a train of ex-LMS non-corridor stock crosses Leyland Road
at Middleforth, with the 18.35 to Preston, on August 17, 1964. *(Alan Castle)*

A grimy Black 5 passes through Middleforth, from Southport to Preston. *(Alan Castle)*

It had always been the objective of the WLR to connect with the ELR at Preston and so gain running powers into Blackburn; this was finally achieved in April 1883, when a triangle of three junctions was created between Cop Lane and the Ribble bridge. The new line passed under the NU and curved southwards to join the ELR at Whitehouse Junction (later, Whitehouse South Junction).

It was now possible for trains travelling from Southport to Blackburn to by-pass Preston by way of Penwortham and Middleforth junctions. Similarly, trains from Preston West Lancashire station could now travel to Blackburn by way of Ribble and Middleforth Junctions. Notwithstanding the tried and tested power of the steam shovel, difficulties were encountered during the construction of embankments and tunneling work beneath the NU tracks, where excavations went down to a depth of 20 ft. and then had to be filled in with some 4000 cubic yards of concrete, to provide a substantial foundation for the new bridge.

Fishergate Hill terminus in 1962, bereft of platforms and the canopy glazing *(G. Harrop)*

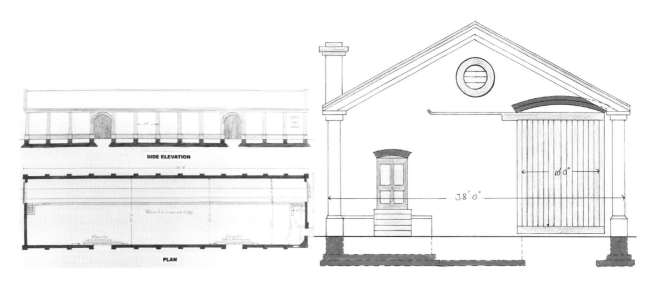

Goods shed, Side elevation & Plan.   Goods shed, End elevation
(Drawings by Author, from WLR Plans courtesy of Mike Norris)

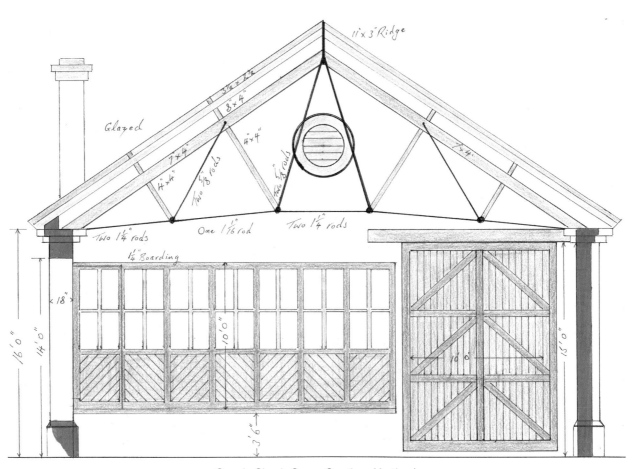

Goods Shed, Cross Section *(Author)*

Ribble Junction box was located on the west side of the line between the Leyland Road and Ribble bridges. It was a McKenzie & Holland design of 1882 with an 18 lever frame. Penwortham Junction box was another McKenzie & Holland design of 1883 with a 16 lever frame. It was closed in 1961 and replaced by a ground frame which controlled the single line section to Fishergate Hill. Middleforth Junction box was located approximately half way between the Leyland Road and Stricklands Lane bridges, where the tracks divided. This was of the same manufacture as the other two and controlled the junction for the curve leading to Fishergate Hill, via Ribble Junction. Following the closure of Preston WL to passengers, the box was removed and replaced by a ground frame. The curve closed completely in 1905.

WEST LANCASHIRE RAILWAY

COMPANY

SPECIAL NOTICE for SATURDAY, August 31st.

BAMBER BRIDGE - SCHOOL LANE - CO-OPERATIVE SOCIETY'S EXCURSION - BAMBER BRIDGE to SOUTHPORT and Back.

		p.m.
Bamber Bridge	Dep.	1.40
Preston Junction	,,	1.44
Whitehouse Junction	Pass	1.46
Middleforth Junction	Pass	1.48
Penwortham Junction	Pass	1.50
Churchtown	Dep.	2.10
Southport	Arr.	2.15
Southport	Dep.	9.0
Preston	Arr.	9.25
Preston	Dep.	9.30
Whitehouse Junction	Pass	9.34
Preston Junction	Dep.	9.36
Bamber Bridge	Arr.	9.40

Probable number: 400.

Tickets to be collected as ordinary.

The train to consist of 2 Carriage Brake Vans, 6 Saloons, 1 Compo, and 2 Thirds.

Preston Chronicle.

39

Financial problems were mounting for the WLR. In 1885 a second appeal was made to the Manchester, Sheffield & Lincolnshire Railway (MS&LR) to help with train workings, but the MS&LR had other, greater commitments pending. Things got worse as a result of failed attempts at further expansion, namely the extension of the line to Blackpool via Preston dock. The company was declared bankrupt and was taken over by the LYR in 1897, who then set about making improvements to the infrastructure and replacing some of the obsolete engines and rolling stock with their own. In 1900, a west to north curve was put in at a point to the east of the NU bridge (Whitehouse West Junction), connecting with the East Lancs line at Whitehouse North Junction. The curve from Middleforth Junction to Ribble Junction was taken out shortly afterwards, and all Southport trains were directed to and from their Butler Street station at Preston, thus making the Preston West Lancashire terminus redundant as far as regular passenger traffic was concerned. It was opened again to passengers for a brief period in 1902, to ease congestion during the Guild Merchant festivities and the station signal box was closed down at the end of that year. From then on, Fishergate Hill served as a goods depot and stock sidings, handling for the most part merchandise to and from the Port of Preston.

The line struggled on for some 46 years until B.R. took over in 1948 for a period of 16 years whereupon, following a recommendation in the Beeching report, the section from Penwortham Junction to Southport was subsequently closed to all traffic on September 6, 1964, after a life of only 82 years. Freight workings ceased altogether at Fishergate Hill on January 22, 1965, the last goods agent being a popular gentleman by the name of James Mason.

FOOTNOTES

[1] Preston Guardian August 1881

[2] ibid.

[3] The Builder, Sept. 1882.

[4] Part of the roof on the Derby Road station at the Southport end, was blown down during a severe gale on November 1, 1882.

Class 08 shunter, D4021, pushes a rake of wagons past the derelict signal box. *(Ivan Stewart)*

CHAPTER THREE

Butler Street Station & Goods Yard

PRESTON

The arrival of the ELR in Preston in 1850, only added to the prevailing state of congestion and confusion at Fishergate (Preston NU) station, which was already deemed to be decrepit, dangerous and wholly inadequate for the purpose which it was intended to serve. There was serious overcrowding on the narrow island platforms and passengers had to risk their lives crossing the tracks on the level when going from one platform to the other. The NU bridge over the Ribble carried two tracks only at that time, which branched out to six north of the park bridge before entering the station, which had two side and three island platforms. Just beyond this point there was a bottleneck in the form of a tunnel with two tracks, which ran beneath Fishergate on a steep gradient.

Following a series of discussions, a proposal was put forward to the effect that the ELR be provided with a safer and more convenient method of access to the west side of the station by means of signals and a level crossing. The NU strongly objected on grounds of safety and the inevitable disruption to their own traffic. The matter was eventually resolved when the NU agreed to build a bridge at the south end of the station and to instruct all passengers to use it as the only permitted method of crossing the tracks. It was also agreed that the ELR should continue to use the east platform. This was approved by the NU in 1855.

The various disputes over track usage and access continued until the station was rebuilt in 1880 and the Butler Street entrance added in 1913 (the EL side having platforms 7, 8 and 9). The two separate entrances served to illustrate the extent to which the management was divided, with both companies having their own station master and staff, a state of affairs which continued to exist until the grouping in 1923. The old NU and EL appellations, however, continued to be used by all members of staff right up to the closure of Butler Street, and are still used to this day, albeit retrospectively, by former railwaymen.

Unidentified Lostock Hall radial tank, at platform 11 with a local train from East Lancashire, circa 1954. The lady with one foot on the engine is a former Butler Street carriage cleaner. *(Courtesy, Ken Roberts)*

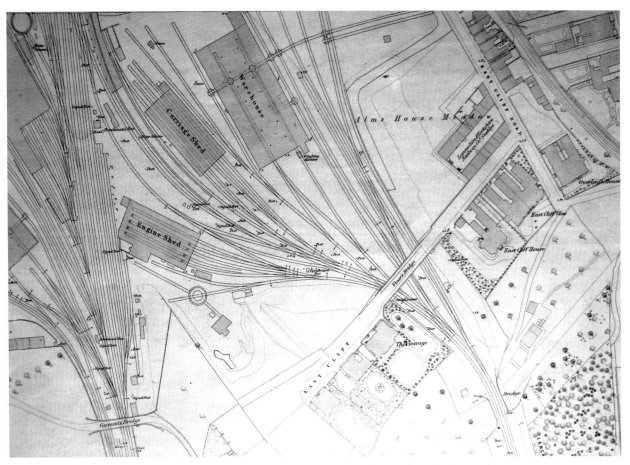

Plan showing 1850's yard layout at Butler Street *(Harris Library)*

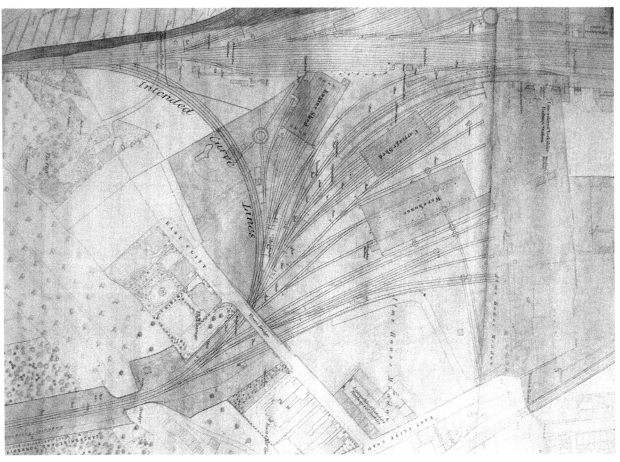

Plan showing yard layout at Butler Street with proposed curve *(British Railways)*

An official joint railway postcard of the rebuilt station at Preston,
with the LYR platforms on the right *(Author's collection)*

The ELR station occupied a small area to the south of the footbridge on the east side platform. The meagre facilities comprised two waiting rooms, a parcel office and an office for the station master; the refreshment room, telegraph office and booking office being the sole responsibility of the NU. The Bolton & Preston and Lancashire & Yorkshire railway companies also had running powers into the station, and access to the NU carriage & wagon shops on Butler Street.

Clearly, this arrangement was wholly inconvenient to say the least, and provision had to be made for a new station and goods yard. After much negotiation, the company purchased a considerable area of land to the south of Fishergate, known as Alms House Meadow, which was bordered on the north side by a large timber yard, served by a branch line from the Preston & Walton Summit tram road. Work began immediately with the construction of a new goods shed, which was a typical ELR single-storey design using brick instead of the traditional stone.

It had a length of 174 ft., a width of 94 ft. and a height of 14 ft. from the top of the rails to the underside of the beams and must have been quite a draughty place as there were eight arched openings on either side; six on the south end and five on the north, the place of a sixth being taken by a two story office building. The side openings were furnished with sliding timber doors and, owing to the width of the piers, the openings at each end were fitted with hinged doors.

The building was covered with three partially-glazed longitudinal gabled roofs; the pinewood queen-post trussing being supported on two rows of seven tubular cast-iron columns (which also served as rainwater down-spouts) and 18 wall corbels. Originally, only two of the six openings (roads 2 and 5, numbering left to right) were served by tracks, which terminated at the end of the building. It was opened to traffic in June 1850 after a delay of some weeks following the collapse of a large section of the masonry during a severe gale in February of that year. The contractor was Samuel Holme of Liverpool, who carried out the work at a cost of £11,000.

Four of the surrounding sidings were connected to a transverse track, which entered the warehouse at the third opening from the rear by way of a series of wagon turntables; there was also a coal yard and cattle dock to the north of the building and a branch to the east of it serving the timber yard. Shortly after the building was opened, the entrance to road 6 was bricked-up and a weigh-bridge office built in front of it; the wagon weigh-bridge itself being built on road 5. These were subsequently removed and the opening reinstated by the LMS in the early 30's.

The company's aptitude for commercial flexibility was demonstrated on Thursday, September 12, 1850, when the Royal North of Lancashire Agricultural Society held its annual show on a field, owned by the Rev. Thursby, close to the ELR station where the newly completed goods shed was made available for the exhibition of prize livestock, farming implements and steam-powered machinery. Later on that day the building served as a venue for the Society's annual dinner, with one or two officers of the railway company as special guests. A similar event took place at the same venue in February of the following year.

North elevation of EL goods shed, with the old fish dock in the right foreground *(Keith Till)*.

The goods agent at that time was Joseph Green; the manager of the goods department, Frederick Broughton, the Station Master, James Cartmell and the main coal merchant was Thomas Barker. The East Lancs warehouse, or Salford EL as it was universally known, was a transhipment shed only, dealing mainly with consignments to and from the Manchester area whereby freight was transferred rapidly from rail to road and vice versa. When the LYR took over, they ran a third track (road 3) into the building in 1882 and a 20 ft. section of the west wall was angled inwards at the south end to make room for a line to the fish dock.

The entrance to road one and its corresponding entrance at the north end were bricked-up, and a timber canopy was built onto the east side of the shed to provide necessary shelter for the loading bays. In early nationalisation days, the north entrance opposite road 2 was bricked-up to allow for the construction of much needed washroom facilities. In busy times when the shed was full, the task of freight handling was carried out in the yard by a method known as 'pramming'. This was originally a name given to a time-honoured maritime practice whereby a flat-bottomed vessel called a pram or lighter, drew alongside a larger ship to load/unload it some distance from the quayside. In railway terms, flat-bed carts and lorries were used to 'pram' goods from the wagons to the shed and vice versa. A carriage shed with 4 through tracks and a bay was built to the west of the goods shed; and lodged up close to the NU tracks was an engine shed with five terminal roads, complete with coaling stage, engineer's shop and turntable.

View of station and yard from Vicar's Bridge in August 1959, with Austerity 90266
returning light to Lostock Hall shed *(Ben Brookesbank)*

The long overdue completion of the new station at Preston in 1880 brought about vast improvements in traffic management for both companies and the LYR was able to provide additional passenger facilities including the construction of up and down platforms and two bays. There was, however, a considerable delay in the reconstruction of the main station, as recorded at the time by Mr. James Armytage C.E. who was borough surveyor for Preston:

'Another effort is going to be made to erect a new railway station in Preston. For many years we have had to put up with a dismal, rickety old structure, improperly termed a railway station, and a short time ago we were relieved by the intelligence that the unworthy building was to be consigned to oblivion, and in its place was to be built one of the finest structures for railway purposes in the north of England. Elaborate and extensive plans were prepared: we inspected them; were well satisfied with them, and rejoiced in the expectation that we should soon be able to boast of a new, commodious and beautiful railway station. A few months ago, the contract was let to a Bolton firm; materials were brought down and the work of destruction commenced. For a few weeks the work proceeded in first class style; then there were signs of a relaxation of exertions, and this was speedily followed by the withdrawal of men and materials. The reason for this strange state of affairs was not publicly known; but it was rumoured that the contractors could not proceed with the work without involving themselves in severe and repeated losses, and they had to perform the forfeiture of their bond, rather than risk the completion of the work at the extraordinary increases in costs to themselves. The precincts of the station have been, and indeed are now in a state of confusion; walls are left half pulled-down; there are incomplete excavations, and there is nothing but chaos. At a meeting of the directors of the railway company held on Saturday, the tender of Messrs. Cooper & Tullis, of Preston, for the erection of the station, was accepted, and we only hope that they may have the honour of completing the much talked-of new station'. (1)

A fine old picture of the Butler Street façade taken around 1921, with a mixed gathering of station staff, and non-uniformed officers. A soldier, who was possibly one of the many railwaymen who signed up during the great war, is in the centre row. The photo was probably taken shortly after the amalgamation of the LYR and LNWR companies, which was never a happy marriage. Of interest is the ornamental wrought-iron border on the glazed canopy with the joint company logo on a panel of glazed white tiles. *(Author's collection).*

The Butler Street station was further extended in 1913 with an up through line and an additional bay. The through line passed beneath the LYR reception buildings, emerging just south of the Fishergate bridge. The numbering of these platforms changed over the years and is covered under the section: Train workings at Butler Street. Beyond the through line was the 'fish mound' platform and behind this, the loading dock for horses, theatrical and circus traffic.

A large five storey warehouse was erected by the LYR in 1884. It measured 210 ft. by 98 ft. and had a deep basement built entirely of blue engineering bricks. The rest of the building was constructed with red Accrington bricks, and the edges of the hoist reveals trimmed with the blue Staffordshire bull-nosed type. It had two longitudinal gabled roofs; the west roof being noted for having the company's name and the building's purpose painted in full title in large white letters across the slates.

There were no tracks within the warehouse and the transfer of goods to and from railway wagons was carried out alongside a canopied bay on the west side. The building was characterised by having four external timber-clad jigger hoists either side, two open jiggers at the rear and one on the left hand side at the front. The contractors were Messrs. Edmund Taylor & Sons of Littleborough, and the work was carried out at a cost of £20,000.

This warehouse dealt mainly with cotton from Liverpool for distribution to Preston's mills. There was also a bonded section for tobacco and alcohol and a section for private rentable storage; these areas were partitioned-off from the cotton and general goods sections by thick walls with wrought-iron fireproof doors. The coal yard was closed down in 1881 to make way for the new development, and all coal handling was transferred to Maudland, Deepdale and Corporation Street.

The Butler Street end of Fishergate tunnel, with the Queens Buildings above *(Harris Museum)*

A new approach road was constructed in 1884, utilising part of the old tramway tunnel. The entrance was at the junction of Charnley Street and the newly constructed Corporation Street (see diagrams), from where a steep declivity ran parallel to the latter street before curving away to the left to run beneath Fishergate and into the yard on a gentler slope.[2] The work was carried out by the Manchester firm of Robert Nowell and supervised by Mr. G.H. Bromley.

The massive, five storey LYR warehouse of 1884 *(Harris Museum)*

The land above the tunnel on Fishergate was subsequently developed by the railway as rentable property, including the Victoria and Albert buildings on the north side and Queen's buildings on the south, where the backs overlooked the yard. The East Lancs. carriage shed was demolished and a new one constructed on the site of the engine shed, which had become redundant following the completion of a new shed at Lostock Hall. The goods agent in 1882 was a Mr S Crompton and the station master, a Mr R. B. Nield.

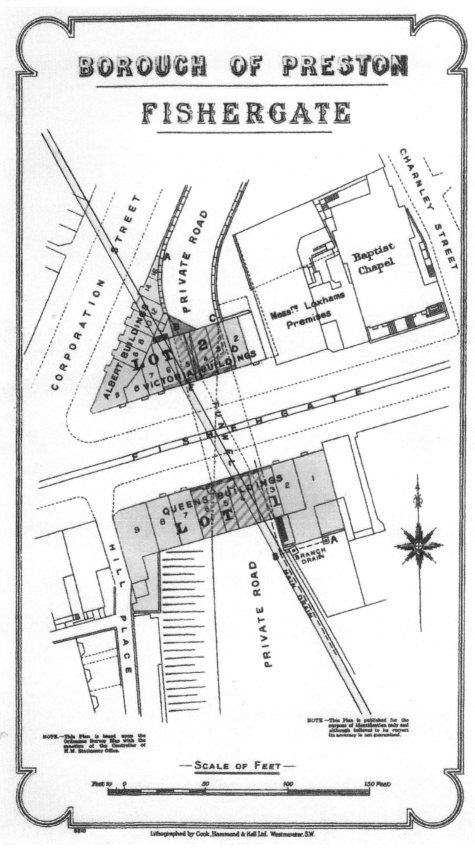

LMS Estates Department plan for 1935, showing Fishergate tunnel and surrounding rented properties. The straight, diagonal line represents the course of the dismantled tram road. *(Author's collection)*

An overhead steam crane was erected on the west side of the LYR warehouse. It had two hoists, one for 7 tons and another for 20 tons maximum capacity. Water was supplied to the boiler and locomotive siphons from a large tank on the west side of Vicar's Bridge. In LMS days the crane was used mainly for handling steel stock and container traffic, with the principle cargo here being bananas from the Geest Company. The banana wagons came up from the docks and were taken round to Butler Street by way of Farington, Lostock Hall and Todd Lane. The steam crane was decommissioned and dismantled in the early BR years, and replaced by an electrically powered type located on the west side of the LYR warehouse.

Ex-LYR 4-4-0, 10129, at platform 11 with the Liverpool portion of the
10.20 from Glasgow, on 14th April 1930. *(Courtesy LCGB, Ken Nunn collection)*

The fish dock adjacent to platform 10 (LMS days) was managed by passenger staff. The train would arrive from Fleetwood and the vans back-shunted into the dock. These trains used to arrive at all times of the day and the fish merchants were always there to double-check the consignments. This part of the yard had other similar appellations: fish mound, fish hillock and fish bay etc. The fishmongers here were Bilsborrow's; Iddon's; Melling's; Mellor's and Taylor's. The fish mound was also used for the shipment of smaller livestock, such as hens, pigeons, greyhounds and young calves which had to be transported in sacks, with their heads sticking out.

Radial tank, 10752, and unidentified class member prepare to leave the carriage
sidings with stock for local stopping trains. *(W.D. Cooper)*

Occupied coffins were also sent from here at the rate of one shilling per mile. A horse dock adjacent to the fish mound was used for the handling of circus and theatrical traffic. Bertram Mills was the main client here and folks lined the streets to watch the elephants walk from the yard to the circus site in line ahead, or Indian file, with tails tied to trunks. Theatrical props arrived in old passenger stock which had been specially converted for that purpose, with seats and bulkheads removed. The Hippodrome on Friargate and the Palace on Tithebarn Street were the main destinations for the props. All circus traffic was transferred to the horse dock at Christian Road in 1950.

Ex-LYR 4-4-0, 10106, waits in the siding for the next local passenger trip. *(Real Photographs Co.)*

The two main watering holes on Butler Street were the Queens at No.1 and the Railway Hotel at No.5. They were always referred to as the top house and bottom house respectively by generations of railway workers. In 1895 a third establishment opened at No.4 known as the Temperance Hotel, the proprietor being a staunch total abstinence lady named Maggie Parry, who was determined to continue the work which had begun in 1832 with Joseph Livesey and a group of Preston artisans.

She played a brave and defiant role between the two male dominated pubs, but landlords Dick Brown of the Railway and John Tattersall of the Queens had little to worry about, as few railwaymen would have darkened her doorstep. It was common knowledge in those days that the railway ran on steam and alcohol, as it continued to do throughout the steam era and a decade or two beyond - minus the steam of course.[3]

In 1890, the LYR drew up plans for a proposed doubling of the tracks from Whitehouse North to Butler Street. Had it gone ahead, the Ribble bridge and the area to the north would have looked very different indeed. Some years before this, Plans were drawn up to connect the E.L. with the N.U. by way of a north/south curve round the base of the Cliff , but nothing came of it.

Retired railwayman Bob Tye of Lostock Hall, joined the railway in 1934 and worked in the parcels office at Butler Street from 1954 to 1973. This is a compendium of the account he gave of day to day working life at the station and yard: By 1950, there were only 2 horse-drawn carts remaining in regular operation. The rest of the road delivery stock comprised six motor lorries including the ubiquitous Scammel Scarab 3-wheel articulated trucks, nicknamed 'Cobs,' after the horses and the new Dennis Pax flat bed lorries which handled the heavier merchandise. The yard staff averaged around 50 men plus 12 clerical staff.

A six-wheeled, double gas-cylinder wagon, No. 317111, which was adapted to carry water
and kept on stand by in case of fire breaking out in locations which
would have been difficult to access by the fire brigade. *(Author's collection)*

The final stages of Butler Street station buildings in the 1970's, before complete demolition. The façade has
had its canopy and BR signage removed to reveal the initials of the pre-nationalisation proprietors.
(Barry Frankland)

Parcels loading bays at Butler Street *(Barry Frankland)*

Rear of station offices from site of former platform and through line *(Barry Frankland)*

The station canopy on Butler Street, just prior to demolition. *(Ivan Stewart)*

Number	Area	Vehicle
1	Fishergate & local district	Horse & Cart
2	Friargate	Horse & Cart
3	Deepdale	Scammel Scarab
4	Fulwood (Outer boundary)	Dennis Pax
5	Plungington	Scammel Scarab
6	Ribbleton	Dennis Pax
7	Ashton	Scammel Scarab
8	Penwortham	Scammel Scarab

From 1948 onwards, all the goods depots in the Preston area came under the supervision of one goods agent, whose office was at Christian Road. The chief clerk and accounts staff also had offices there. The forwarding, delivery, warehouse and cartage offices were at Butler Street.

Destination	Delivery	Destination	Delivery
Ashton-under-Lyme	Next Day	Hull	Next Day
Blackburn	Next Day	Leeds	Next Day
Blackpool	Next Day	Liverpool	Next Day
Bolton	Next Day	Newcastle	2nd Day
Bradford	Next Day	Oldham	Next Day
Burnley	Next Day	Ormskirk	Next Day
Bury	Next Day	Rochdale	Next Day
Chorley	Next Day	Sheffield	2nd Day
Fleetwood	Next Day	Southport	Next Day
Gateshead	2nd Day	Stockton	2nd Day
Huddersfield	Next Day	York	2nd Day

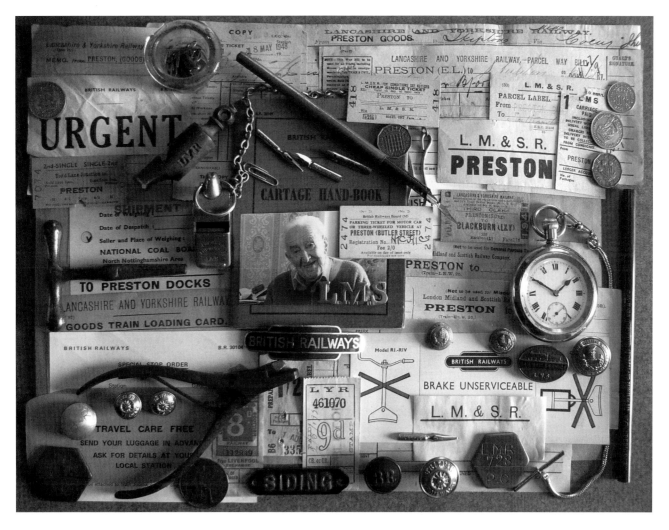

A collection of ephemera and other items relating to Butler Street station.
Where the footplate crews handled tons of coal and gallons of water, the clerical staff had to scribble their way through tons of paper and gallons of ink. There is a countless variety of documents, labels and print-outs pertaining to every aspect of railway operation. The Maestro himself, Bob Tye, is in the centre of the picture.
(Author's collection)

Handling passenger & parcels traffic in BR days

There were two ticket windows in the booking office, one for ordinary services and another for the workmen's trains to Leyland Royal Ordnance Factory (ROF), which was open from 05.30 to 09.00 hrs. only. The glass-roofed parcels office was the busiest department at the station with a staff of 6 working a three shift system. A lot of business came from the mail order companies, such as Dash & Horsefold, Brian Mills and Peter Craig and the office also handled the West Lancashire racing pigeon specials.

The baskets were taken over to the yard at Corporation Street, where the pigeons were released. Later on in the 70's, they were released between Whitehouse North and South junctions, where they were well away from the overhead wires. There was also a regular shipment of day old duck chicks at the rate of 400 boxes per week from Will Bradley's at Broughton to the Bernard Matthews factory at Norwich, from platform 9. All deliveries were finished by 16.00 hrs., then it was collections only and the average consignment was 250 parcels per day.

There was always a spate of activity when the early newspaper trains arrived. Pemberton, Heywood and W H Smith were the main wholesalers, the latter having a warehouse at the foot of Butler Street, and delivery drivers were often bribed with cigarettes to give priority to certain wholesalers.

Night Mail.

GENERAL POST OFFICE.

His Grace the Duke of NORFOLK, K.G., Postmaster-General.

PRESTON and BURNLEY Time Bill.

Mail Messenger's Remarks as to Delays, &c.		Proper Times		Actual Times		P.O. Work completed at		SUNDAY WORKING	
		H.	M.	H.	M.	H.	M.		
	Date 189 .								
		A.M.						A.M.	
	Down Night Mail ....arr.	1	18					1	18
	Preston Post-Office ....dep.	1	45					1	20
	Preston Railway Station..dep.	2	30					2	15
	Monday....	2	15						
	Bamber Bridge ......arr.	2	48					2	50
	Monday....	2	35						
	Blackburn ....arr.	3	18					2	55
	Monday....	2	55						
	Accrington ....arr.	3	40					3	30
	Monday....	3	25						
	Burnley (Mr. Road) ....arr.	4	0					4	0
	Monday (Bank Top)..	4	10						
	Burnley Post-Office.. . arr.	4	15					4	15
	Monday....	4	25						

Lancashire and Yorkshire Railway.

T. E. SIFTON, Inspector-General of Mails.

The Messenger in charge of the Mail must report on this Time Bill:—1st. The cause of any Delay. 2nd. The failure of any Junction. 3rd. The discontinuance of any Stops included in the Bill, or the commencement of any additional Stops; any alteration in the Time allowed between the Stations. 4th. He must enter all Remarks in the proper Column, and opposite or between the Stations to which they refer.

G & S 3I [5867] 500 11/96c

GPO time bill for Preston & Burnley night mail. *(Mike Atherton archive)*

Every station had its own number: Euston, No.1, Watford, No.2, Northampton No.4, Rugby, No.5, Birmingham, No.6, Wolverhampton, No.7, Nuneaton, No.8, Stafford, No.9 and Crewe, No.13. When a parcel arrived at the office, it was booked, weighed, charged and numbered. If it was under contract it would have a ledger label. Ledger 1 was next day and ledger 2 second day. The parcel would then be chalked with a sort code and sent down in the lift to platform 9; from there they were taken to platform 5 and the 'iron cage' on platform 6, from where the majority of parcels were trans-shipped."

Retired railwayman, Ernie Tyrer, began working at Butler Street goods yard in June 1951, when he was 16 years of age. His railway career was subject to a brief interruption in June 1953, when he was called up for national service. He returned to Butler Street in 1955 and was later transferred to Christian Road, where he stayed for a couple of years before being transferred again, this time to the Estates Dept. The following is a brief account of his time in the goods yard, told in his own words:

'I was a delivery clerk, working 5.30 am. to 2 pm. and my job was primarily to book out the delivery drivers who took the goods to firms and individuals in Preston and the surrounding areas. The offices were in a two storey building of domestic scale, attached to the northern end of the (Salford) goods warehouse; we were on the ground floor and shipping was on the first, the hours worked here being from 1 pm. to 9 pm. The warehouse was a huge building with a large platform running along one edge. On the outside of this was a siding, from which goods were unloaded onto the platform, and on the other side of the platform were rows of trailers waiting to be loaded for delivery. Because the warehouse was so large, it was used as a dumping place for broken trailers, old harnesses and all manner of stuff. There was another warehouse called the 'Stock Warehouse' (LYR 5-storey building), used for the storage of cattle food and grain, mainly for BOCM (British Oil & Cake Mills). I used to be a bit scared of this warehouse, as the men who worked in the yard told hair-raising stories of the rats which lurked therein.

Just past the Stock Warehouse was a cartage office and a weigh-bridge, run by a chap called Wally(?) Bennett (who died quite young from leukemia), and beyond that was the tunnel which led under Fishergate and came out in Corporation Street. All rural deliveries were made by motor, in the form of three-wheeled tractor units pulling trailers, but deliveries in Preston were by horse-drawn carts, which were also used for trans-shipping goods around the yard. The horse drivers were tough men, whose protection from the rain usually consisted of an old sack tied around their shoulders.

Their working conditions were grisly, with no amenities other than an unheated cabin to brew up in, and the most awesomely awful toilets located at the north end of the warehouse. These were shared with office staff, and often one would be faced with three or four horses tied up outside the toilet. It was surprising how the urge to go diminished when faced with the prospect of shoving your way past their huge backsides, and meeting their malevolent gaze as they turned their heads to look at you.

The offices consisted of one large room with high desks and stools around the walls, with one ordinary desk in the middle for the boss. He was a man called Jack Worsley, whom I worshiped. His wife used to carefully pack up a lunch for him, which he invariably gave to me and which I ate with the appetite of a healthy 16 year old. I was a keen cyclist then, a passion which I shared with another clerk, Jimmy Potter, who was quite a bit older than me. Other names I remember are Fred Southern, another clerk in his 20's and Freddie Spencer, the yard foreman, who used to shave a bit off a plug of twist tobacco and chew it. Bob Gardner was in charge of the Stock Warehouse, an older man who was very kind to me.

British Railways enamel door plates from Butler Street

Another of the delivery clerks was 'Flash', who was about my age but had escaped national service. He was a nice lad, and the butt of a lot of kidding from the drivers and yard workers, something I was lucky enough to miss. The office was heated by one open fire, so those parts furthest from it were freezing. Coal was scarce (it was only six years after the end of the war), so I used to take the scuttle and walk the 'four-foot' to see what had dropped from the engines. We had two trains a day, one from Brindle Heath, near Manchester and one from Rose Grove, near Burnley.

I used to take my scuttle and scrounge coal off the firemen when the trains came in. After the rush of getting the carters out in the morning, I spent most of the day fielding telephone calls and watching wagons being shunted around to make up a train which left at night, I think, for Carlisle. This period was not long after nationalisation and there was still a lot of loyalty to the old companies. These were the L&Y and the L&NW lines, and pre-date the 1921 amalgamation, but were still referred to. I think the companies had different conditions which were carried forward on nationalisation.

Butler Street was the main depot for the handling of 'full loads', these would consist of a single wagon, several wagons or even a complete train-load of goods for one consignee. The regular cargo here comprised steel billets and joists etc. for one of the main steel stockholders in the town. The steel was delivered to the yard on bogie-bolster wagons, which were long flatbeds with a 4-wheeled bogie at either end, usually, but not always, with fitted brakes (it was surprising how many wagons were not fitted with the continuous vacuum brake in those days). Local contractor, Chris Miller, used to send his low-loader vehicles to collect the steel when the wagons had been shunted under the gantry crane. There was only one female member of staff in the yard, a lovely lady called Alice (I never discovered her surname). She was a 'number snatcher' and her job was to walk along the rakes of wagons in the yard, recording the numbers, types and stations of origin.

She would appear in the office with a handful of wagon labels, on which she had written these details. Considering the rough environment in which she worked, she was treated with a great deal of respect.'

Jubilee, 45584 North West Frontier, prepares to leave the station
with a parcels train. *(Arthur Haymes)*

On October 28, 1971, a meeting was held at Preston to outline the proposed withdrawal of all full-load traffic from Butler Street and the complete closure of the depot. The proposal was made in pursuance of the British Railways Board (BRB) policy to concentrate traffic at fewer depots in order to reduce terminal operating costs. During the course of that year, the depot lost 15 regular and high revenue customers, including mail order companies, electrical wholesalers and steel stock-holders. The daily average for wagons was down to 16, each with an average load of 10 tons. The once numerous yard staff had dwindled down to four clerical officers: one C.O.3, one C.O.2 and two C.O 1 's, one grade B supervisor, one senior railman, four leading railmen and three ordinary railmen.

Butler Street was closed in December 1971 together with Christian Road, and all freight handling was transferred to Blackburn. The Passenger station at Butler Street was closed on May 1, 1971, but the parcels office remained open until 1976, when all business was transferred to the old platform one (horse dock), adjacent to Christian Road, which later incorporated the Red Star parcels service.

Train workings at Butler Street

Following the rebuilding of Preston station the East Lancs. section settled down to a recognisable traffic pattern which remained more or less constant until closure. The following table serves to illustrate how the platform numbering had changed over the years.

Early LYR Days	Later LYR & LMS days	Later BR days	Description
	Platform 7	Platform 7	Up Loop line
Platform 3	Platform 8	Platform 8	Down main line
Platform 4	Platform 9	Platform 9	Up main line
	Platform 10	Platform 13	Up through line
No. 1 Bay	Platform 11	Platform 10	Bay platform with run in loop and engine release
No. 2 Bay	Platform 12	Platform 11	Dead end bay
	Platform 13	Platform 12	Dead end bay

Class 4P compound, 41186 of Southport shed, waits at platform 13 with a local train for the return trip, in October 1956. The station lamp ladders have been commandeered for the replacement of the canvas bag on the water crane. *(Real Photographs Co.)*

Typical Passenger train services working through Preston East Lancs

Of these workings probably best known are those between the North and Blackpool (which included many summer excursions), for example the 2 pm Blackpool North to Glasgow Central, reporting number 277, a Saturdays only service which would pass through Preston NU platform 2 at 2.34 pm.

heading south, taking Farington Curve Junction to Lostock Hall and then on to Preston Junction to pass through the east side of Preston station via platform 8 at 2.40 pm. (some 25 minutes later) to stop and change enginemen. This process allowed bi-directional traffic without the need for engine changes at Preston and minimising delays to north/south traffic (exactly the problem that the NU wanted to avoid all those years earlier). The carriage shed adjacent to the station provided facilities for the large number of services starting and terminating at Preston. Other support facilities included carriage and wagon repair shop with smithy and workshops for gas fitters, plumbers, joiners and painters, all located close to the turntable.

Blackpool Dreadnought, 10448, eases round the curve on platform 9 with
a train of empty coal wagons for West Yorkshire. *(W. D. Cooper)*

The crew of Lostock Hall Fairburn tank, 42187 appear to be preoccupied with something going on
across the way, as they wait for the 'off' with a fast train to Liverpool Exchange. *(Chris Spring)*

Lostock Hall Fairburn, 42296, awaits her next turn of duty,
while stablemate, 42425 shunts the carriage sidings, on 7th April 1964.
The magnificent Park Hotel building dominates the background. *(Chris Spring)*

Fowler 4P tank, 42369 of Southport shed, takes five in No.13 bay on 18th June 1964.
Note the adjacent fish dock, with weighing machines and fish crates. *(Chris Spring)*

Freight Services

Of the freight services in and out of Butler Street goods yard many consisted of short 'Trip' workings where a locomotive would transfer wagons between adjacent yards. The locomotives on these workings would carry a disc with the working number on the buffer beam much like a reporting number for a service train; this was nicknamed the 'Target' number.

No.21 - PRESTON BUTLER STREET SHUNT Class 2 Freight Tank Engine						
5.50 a.m. MO to 8.18 p.m. SO						
			arr. **MO**	dep. **MO**		
			a.m.	a.m.		
Lostock Hall Shed				5.50 L.E.		
Preston Butler St.			5.58			
Shunts to 7.0 p.m. And works						
	arr.	dep.			arr.	dep.
	p.m.	p.m.			p.m.	p.m.
Preston Butler St.		7.2	Ribble Sidings		8.0	8.10 L.E.
Lostock Hall	7.15	7.40	Lostock Hall Shed		8.18	
Test Vacuum Stock as required						

No. 8 - Class 7 Freight Engine (G.2.)						
5.50 a.m. MO to 6.00 a.m. Sundays						
Work as required to and from Preston Dock also works the following trips: (Engine to be facing south and sent to shed at suitable time for coal)						
			arr.	dep.		
			p.m.	p.m.		
		Preston Dock		4.45 **A**		
		N.U. Yard	4.55	5.30		
		Preston Dock	5.50	6.20 **B**		
		Ribble Sidings	6.30			
	arr. **MO**	dep. **MO**			arr. **MX**	dep. **MX**
	a.m.	a.m.			a.m.	a.m.
Preston Shed		5.55 L.E.*	N.U.Yard			3.15
N.U.Yard	6.0	6.12	Preston E.L.		3.35	4.30 E&B
Preston E.L.	6.36	7.10 E&B	Ribble Sidings		5.0	
Ribble Sidings	7.43					
A - South Traffic						
B - North Traffic						
* No. 13 Trip Light Engine coupled to Ribble Sidings **MO**						

No.30 - Class 3 Freight Engine				
Preston Butler St.	10.30			
			a.m.	
		Farington Jn.	12.32	
			Shunt	
			a.m.	
		Farington Jn.	3.30 L.E.	
		Lostock Hall Shed	3.35	

Trip workings dealt mainly with traffic to and from Lostock Hall, Ribble Sidings and Bamber Bridge, much of it overnight. They were given a letter prefix in the working timetables which would indicate the home shed of the engine: typically 'P' for Preston shed or 'L' for Lostock Hall. There seems to be slight confusion over trip 50, it's listed as 'F50' in the trip working instructions and 'B50' in the working timetables, but the locomotive does visit both Fleetwood and Blackpool North shed, so can be excused! As well as trip workings a number of trains were booked to stop or start from Butler Street.

Unnumbered Local Trips
2.0 a.m. (**MX**) Lostock Hall Sidings to Preston (Butler Street).
5.40 a.m. (**MO**) Preston (Butler Street) to Ribble Sidings.

No. F.50 KIRKHAM SHUNT
Engine not specified

6.10 a.m. to 11.10 a.m. MO
6.0 a.m. to 11.15 a.m. MSX
6.0 a.m. to as required SO

After working 2.40 a.m. **MX** Wyre dock to Preston (Butler St.)

	arr. **MO** a.m.	dep. **MO** a.m.		arr. p.m.	dep. p.m.	arr. **MX** a.m.	dep. **MX** a.m.
Fleetwood Shed		6.10 L.E.	Preston (Butler St.)				6.0 L.E.
Kirkham	6.30		Kirkham			6.20	
	Shunt					Shunt	
Kirkham		11.55 L.E.	Kirkham				10.55 L.E.
Blackpool N. Shed	11.10		Fleetwood			11.15	

2-4-2 tank, 10953 of Accrington shed, arrives with a local train. The 140ft span of Vicar's Bridge is shown to good effect in the background. *(Noel Coates)*

Preston East Lancs. Goods signal box was a Saxby & Farmer type 6 brick structure, built in 1873 and measured 32 ft. x 14 ft. with a platform elevation of 10 ft. From 1927 up to closure it had a 56 lever LYR frame with a capacity for 60, and controlled traffic for the EL side of the station, including the carriage sidings and Butler Street yard; it also electrically controlled a ground frame which in turn operated the switches for a siding at the fish mound, adjacent to platform 13. Its official title was Fish Dock G.F., and comprised a 4-lever LYR frame contained within a wooden hut measuring 6 ft. 9 ins. x 4 ft.

Britannia pacific, 70012 John of Gaunt, minus nameplates, reverses over the points
across from the East Lancs Goods signal box, circa 1966. *(Peter Ditchfield)*

At the north end of the station, the up and down main lines (platforms 8 and 9) and the up loop line (platform 7) were controlled from Preston No.3 box, whereas the up through (No.10 platform in LMS days) was controlled by the No.4 box, all complying with 'station yard working', which is a form of permissive block, allowing more than one train in the section between signal boxes at one time, provided they are brought to a stand and called-on before entering a section. [3] This generally allowed vehicles to be attached or detached from trains or, in some cases, when two workings were to be combined.

The up and down lines from EL Goods to Whitehouse North Junction were subject to absolute block and there was a speed limit of 10 m.p.h. between the centre of Preston station and the Ribble viaduct. There were special instructions in place at Preston EL. The sectional appendix states: *'When a bay platform is not clear to the buffers a train requiring to enter such platform line will be brought to a stand at the down outer home signal at goods yard box, and drivers of trains brought to a stand at those signals must understand when the signal is taken off, as the line may not be clear to the buffer stops, and must have their trains thoroughly under control and be prepared to stop short of any obstruction.'*

Also: *'Down and up passenger and empty coaching stock trains not booked to stop at Preston station, requiring relief or conductors must stop at E. L. goods yard box. Trainmen must report to the Yard Foreman at Preston E. L., who will advise the men of the approach of the train they have to work. The signalman at E. L. Goods Yard box must advise the Signalman at No.5 box when up trains require conductors or relief.'* [4]

The 'EL' up and down main lines (platforms 8 and 9) were utilised in the 1972 remodelling of Preston station and now form platform 6 and a goods loop (both bi-directional) under the control of Preston Power Signal Box (PSB).

Hughes-Fowler 5MT 2-6-0 Crab, 42869, arriving at Butler Street with a local stopping train *(Arthur Haymes)*

This is how the E.L. passenger service looked in the twilight years:
Diesel multiple units are seen here working the Preston - Colne service
on 30th March 1970. *(J .S. Hancock)*

FOOTNOTES

Butler Street goods yard & station

(1) Preston Guardian, July 5, 1873.

(2) This road now serves the car park for the Fishergate shopping centre.

(3) Butler Street was quite a hive of activity from the 1830's onwards: apart from the top and bottom houses, there were the Stevenson's Tavern, adjacent to the EL station; and the North Union Hotel at the top of the street, across from the Queens. Bleazard's Oyster saloon was located somewhere half-way down the street; and there was Newsome's Hippodrome and Circus, specialising in horse and pony acts, which occupied a large building adjacent to the goods yard. The Victoria Hotel on Fishergate, directly across from the entrance to Butler Street, was a very popular establishment in its time, and highly recommended by the railway companies.

Train workings at Butler Street

(1) Table of maintenance & working of junction, May 1910, shows bays still numbered as 1 & 2. (Harris Museum)

(2) Platforms 7, 8 and 9 were mentioned in a 1903 accident report; this suggests they were renumbered after the widening of 1903. The bays 1 & 2 were assumed to have been renumbered after the 1913 building work. The LMS platform numbering was described in the Railway Magazine in May 1926; this was still in place in the LMS working timetable for 1947 and photographs from 1952.

(3) This was usually by a miniature arm mounted below the main section starting signal.

(4) General appendix to the working time-tables, with sectional appendix. Central Division, March 1937. LMS.

LYR Barton Wright 4-4-0, No. 675 Duchess of Albany, at Butler Street, circa 1885. *(Harris Museum)*

CHAPTER FOUR

The Railway Stables at East Cliff

For many years, horses were used extensively for carting and shunting duties at Preston. These were the Shire or Draught horses with an average height of 17 hands (or 5 ft. 10 ins. to the withers) and a girth of 6 ft. to 8 ft. By 1900 there were over 60 horses employed at Butler Street alone. They were well cared-for and examined regularly by trained horse inspectors and veterinary surgeons. [1] When out on the road they looked resplendent in their polished harness gear, embellished here and there with ornamental brasses; some of the finer stallions went on to win awards at local agricultural shows. Their hooves were fitted with special iron shoes, fashioned with toe-pieces and 'hammered' heels, which provided a firm grip in the spaces between the setts when going uphill.

EAST LANCASHIRE RAILWAY.

TO BUILDERS AND CONTRACTORS.

The Directors of this Company are prepared to receive tenders for the erection of STABLES, to contain stalls for 29 horses, two loose boxes, stable keeper's house and other conveniences at the Preston station. Plans and specifications may be seen on application to Mr. Green, East Lancashire Goods Warehouse, Preston Station. Sealed tenders addressed to the undersigned, will be received on or before the 25th day of November next.

By order,
Myles Fenton, Secretary

Preston Station, November 5th, 1856.

Preston Guardian, November 15th 1856

The stables serving the East Lancs yard were constructed in 1856 on elevated land at the junction of East Cliff and East Cliff Road, close to the site of the future Park Hotel. The architect was a Mr J. Perring and the contract was awarded to the Preston firm of Cooper & Tullis, who carried out a considerable amount of work for the railway companies in the Preston area, including the rebuilding of Fishergate and Butler Street stations. The buildings were laid out in the form of a rhomboid, with the East Cliff Road side (east elevation) measuring 112 ft.; the East Cliff (south elevation) 240 ft.; the west elevation, 98 ft. and the north elevation, 234 ft. The main gateway on East Cliff Road was flanked by two imposing two storey buildings, each boasting decorative masonry work on the walls and chimney stacks. The building on the right provided living quarters for the head horse keeper and his family and the one opposite had a second floor apartment for the foreman and a staff mess room below. A gateway on the north side led to the goods yard by way of a steep slope. Originally there was provision for 30 horses; increasing to 63 in 1884, with a further extension in 1896. Other facilities within the compound included a farrier's shop with forge; hay and fodder stores and a harness room with accommodation for leather aprons, nose-bags and buckets. The heavier and more specialised carter's equipment such as chain, rope, sack-trucks, grab-hooks, lamps and lamp oil would have been stored in the goods yard. Each stable section had a height of 9 ft. 8 ins. with a spacious hay-loft above, complete with ventilator and skylight. There was through access to all the hay-lofts which were reached by way of an external staircase. Each stall had a manger and earthenware drinking trough and the floor comprised cambered stone setts with drainage channel and grate.

The extension plans for 1884 made provision for part of the stall floors to be lined with 4 ins. x 4 ins. x 3 ins. oak blocks, as this was the best way of absorbing horse-piss and allowed for a non-slip surface. A similar practice was carried out in goods sheds, especially where there were occupational premises located directly beneath the carting and stable areas; a good example here was the smaller of the Great Northern goods warehouses at Deansgate in Manchester. Sadly this building has been demolished, but many of the oak blocks were salvaged and used to pave the entrance to the G-Mex building.

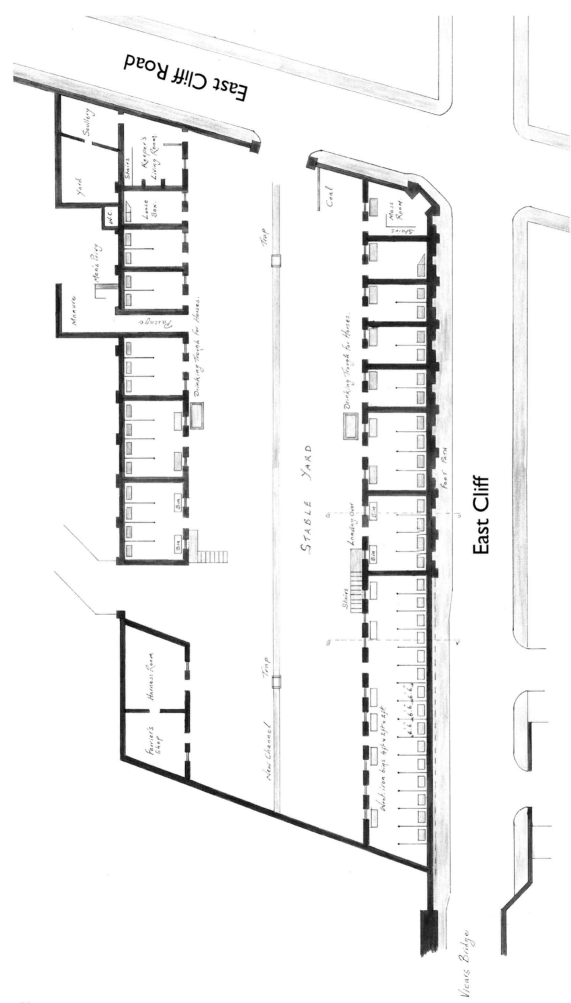

Main plan of stable buildings, 1884
(Drawings by author from original ELR & LYR plans. Courtesy Greater Manchester County Record Office)

East Cliff

Level of East Cliffe Road
Level of Stable floor and yard

South elevation

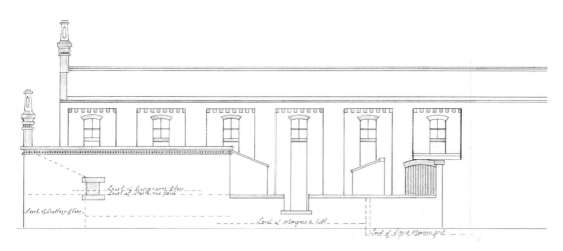

Level of living room floor
Level of Path and yard

Level of Stabling floor

Level of Mangers & Sill

Level of Liquid Manure pit

North elevation

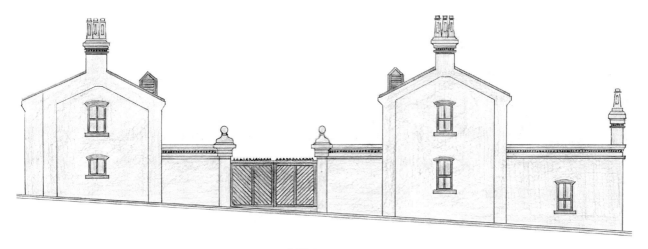

East Cliff Road Elevation

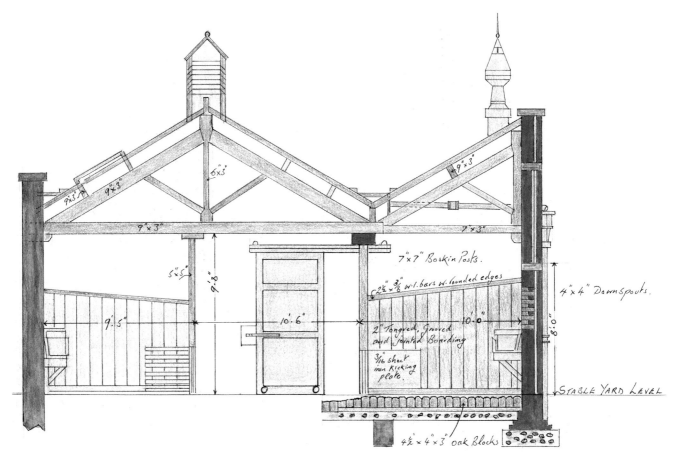

Cross section on line AB

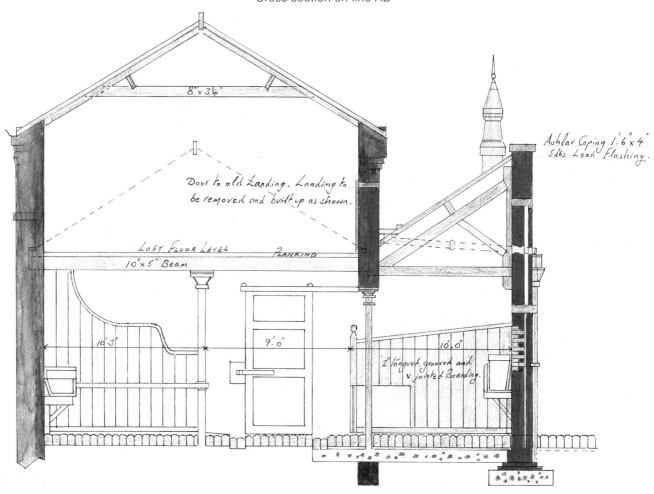

Cross section on line CD

Additional stabling at East Cliff

Owing to the steep climb out of Butler Street each heavily laden horse-drawn cart was assisted by a chain or trace horse in front. A Police officer would be on duty at the top of the hill to control the traffic and allow carts to join the main road on Fishergate. The horses were quite intelligent and soon got used to the Policeman's hand signals and always stopped without any prompting from the carter when the Policeman held his right hand up. One day, when waiting for the right of way at the top of Butler Street, veteran carter, Jimmy Hamer, nipped round to the back of the cart to make sure he'd secured the tailgate. While he was doing this, the Policeman, not noticing the cart was driver-less, waved it on. The horse, who was called Dolly, acknowledged the signal and set off, leaving Jack behind. There was no cause for concern, as Dolly knew exactly where she was going. She turned right and headed east up Fishergate until she reached a certain confectioner's shop. This was the first port of call and she knew the proprietor always had a freshly baked bun for her. One day the proprietor was absent, but Dolly wouldn't budge until she got her bun. Jimmy had to get his hand down and pay for one.

Retired Police Officer, Cliff Cornwell who regularly controlled traffic at the top of Christian Road and Corporation Street, recalled the time he gave chase to a runaway horse and cart in 1949. *"I saw a horse, pulling one of the covered parcels carts, come plodding out of Cheapside without a driver, and cross Fishergate into Glover's Court. I ran up to the cart and tried to apply the brake, but the horse bolted and charged down the street narrowly missing a ladder and rubble-chute on the left hand side. I managed to catch up with it and seeing that the tailgate was down, jumped up on to the back. I clambered over a pile of parcels, some of which were falling onto the road, and fought my way to the front. When I got there I noticed that the reins were dragging along the cobble stones. Fortunately, I found an iron hook on the foot-board and was about to fish the reins up with it, when the cart turned sharply across the busy Avenham Lane.*

I eventually managed to recover the reins and, holding them tight and level as I had seen done on so many Westerns, managed to bring the cart to a stand-still on East Cliff, only yards from Butler Street yard. As I was applying the brake, the driver and his mate came dashing up, carrying some of the fallen parcels with them. They were running late with the Cheapside deliveries that morning and the horse must have got to thinking it was time to go home, so off she went." What treasures we have lost in the name of progress!

The following excerpt is from the memoirs of the late Arthur Eric Crook (1917 – 1997), on his reflections of the working horses in Preston: *"I think the last to go were the railway horses, magnificent shires, who delivered parcels from Butler Street to the public. The big heavy carts were loaded up and then a couple of those mighty beasts, on command, would lean forward to take the strain until the wheels moved slightly, and not until then did they move their feet. No sudden dash forward to move their heavy burden, just a gradual lean forward into their collars, which would slowly tighten the haulin' and britchin' chains. Once the wheels started to roll, off they went and the driver would jump up on the front and grab the reins. It seemed a simple operation, but they were moving tons of freight and the cobbled streets helped the horses to gain a foothold. In frosty weather small spiked inserts (frost cogs) were fitted into the shoes to help them maintain a steady gait and prevent them from slipping. The stone setts on the station approach at Fishergate and Butler Street remained in situ long after the main thoroughfares in Preston had been re-surfaced with tarmac, and for some time after the last railway horse had retired."*

Ernie Tyrer, relates his memories of the railway horses during his time at the East Lancs yard: *"All the yard was cobbled to allow the horses a good footing, but sometimes the slope up Butler Street was too much if the trailer was heavily laden. At this point a call went out for the chain horse, which was led from Christian Road and harnessed in front. The trailer was then pulled up the slope double-headed. The horses were a feature of the yard: huge beasts with feet like dinner plates. Sometimes one of them would be spooked while working in the yard and run wild with the trailer swinging behind it, sending parcels and bales flying in all directions. It was advisable to keep out of the way of such incidents. The horses were stabled in East Cliff, and I well remember a driver called Harry Messenger, a nice guy, who had a tendency to look upon the wine while it was red on a Saturday night. His wife would refuse to allow him into the house, so he would occasionally sleep in the stables with the horses. He said it was always nice and warm in the straw. When I returned from the army, Harry was still there, but had found religion and regretted his past misdeeds. He used to exude pamphlets from all pockets if you gave him the slightest encouragement, but he was still a grand chap."*

EAST LANCASHIRE RAILWAY

CONTRACTS FOR HAY AND STRAW

The Directors of the East Lancashire Railway are prepared to receive Tenders for the supply of good, sound and sweet Meadow Hay (old and new in equal proportion), and sound Wheat Straw, delivered at any of their stations in quantities as may from time to time be required during the ensuing six months. It is calculated that the weekly consumption of hay will be about four tons, and straw about two tons. Payment to be made monthly.

Sealed Tenders endorsed.- Tenders for "Hay and straw", to be addressed to me on or before Monday, the 8th proximo; any further information may be obtained on application to

C.W. EBORALL.

General Manager's Office, Bury.
28th July, 1853.

Preston Guardian, 1853

Old Anglo-Saxon and pagan traditions continued throughout the Victorian era in Preston, and one such festivity was the May Day procession which included a string of railway horses. At 8.30 am on Thursday, May 1, 1862, some 30 horses, each one accompanied by its driver, left the Lancashire & Yorkshire Railway stables on East Cliff Road and walked up Chapel Street to join the main procession on Fishergate; and from here they proceeded along Church Street, Park Road, Moor Lane and Friargate.

The first 5 horses were splendid greys and the finest in the company; they were followed by 4 equally fine chestnuts; the rest of the number being browns, bays and blacks.

Each driver had worked hard to decorate his horse with great taste in honour of that hallowed May morning: the highly polished harnesses and brasses gleamed in the sunlight amid a profusion of floral adornments, bouquets and streamers of gaily coloured ribbons. The decoration was both elaborate and tasteful and did the utmost credit to the drivers, who were themselves dressed in the smartest style. The procession was watched on its course by a large number of people; and the horses and their drivers were observed with interest as they went about the streets during the day in the ordinary course of their business, still wearing the decorations that had graced the morning procession. The driver who took first honours was Mr. W. Grimbelston, with Mr. J. Halliwell taking second. [2]

The arrival of the steam lorry in the 1890's made little or no difference to the number of horses employed on the railway, but a noticeable thinning of the ranks began in the early 1920's when thousands of wartime production motor lorries became available at affordable prices. This also heralded the beginning of a long decline in the railway goods service. [3] By 1950 only two horse-drawn carts remained in regular service at Preston (mentioned in chapter three) and shunting with horses had finished altogether.

The stables at East Cliff were closed that same year, the horses and equipment being transferred across the NU tracks to Christian Road. The buildings were then modified to accommodate railway motor vehicles for repairs and routine maintenance purposes; but as the freight service declined over the years they were rented out by BR for private commercial use and later fell into a state of disuse and dereliction. They were subsequently demolished in the late 1960's and the site is now used as a private car park. Much of the original stable flooring with cambered setts, wrought iron partition and 'Boskin-post' bases were still visible up to the end of 2009, when the site was tarmacked over.

Stable floor detail *(Author)*

LYR horse brass

FOOTNOTES

(1) The cost of feeding a horse at the turn of the century was around £50.00 per annum. They were fed for the most part on bran, hay, straw, oats, oatmeal, carrots, turnips and linseed. During particularly cold and wet weather, they were protected by wool-lined canvas coats.

(2) Preston Guardian, 3rd May 1862.

(3) Serious road competition with railway passenger traffic in the Preston area began with the introduction of local bus services in 1910, and the commencement of county services following the establishment of Ribble Motor Services in 1919.

CHAPTER FIVE

The Park Hotel Preston

Aerial view of the south end of Preston station in 1930, with the Park Hotel in the centre.
Note the scaffolding on the piers of the EL Ribble bridge and stationary wagons on the south bank,
indicating that work had almost been completed on the new spans. *(Courtesy, Winter & Kidson)*

The 1880's saw a considerable amount of building development and extension work on the railway infrastructure around Preston. One such contract, a joint venture between the London & North Western Railway (LNWR) and the LYR companies, was for the construction of a large and impressive hotel, so designed as to meet the needs of those travelling on the railway. A favourable site was decided upon in 1877 and tenders invited for the design and construction of the 'New Station Hotel.'

The Park Hotel, as it came to be called, was completed in time for the Guild week in 1882. The architect, Mr. T. Mitchell F.R.I.B.A. of Oldham, was aptly awarded the sum of £200. as first prize in an open competition for the best design and the contract was given to the Manchester firm of R. Neill & Sons at a cost of £40,000; this was for the building only and did not include furniture and fittings. The construction work was supervised by Mr. J. B. Stanley of Euston. The hotel was appropriately situated between the running lines of both companies on an elevated parcel of land known as the Cliff, the site having been purchased from the prominent German family of Preston.[1] Facing south-east, the front of the hotel commanded a panoramic view of the Avenham and Miller parks and the beautiful countryside beyond; it also overlooked a promenade, some 400 ft. long and 18 ft wide, from where the sloping gardens and pathways of the park below could be accessed. A roofed and glazed footbridge once connected the hotel with the LNWR's main island platform; the guests being greeted here by liveried porters and escorted to the primary reception hall on the East Cliffe side. This was quite a spacious and handsome structure: the floor was finished with ornamental octagonal tiles, and the windows glazed with tinted cathedral glass. From here, access to the main building was by way of a glazed and roofed corridor, similarly paved, and having glazed tiles on the walls. It was 180 ft. in length and 8ft. in width, being squarely intersected by a 24 ft. wide cab or carriage-way adjacent to the building, and continued into the hotel's main reception hall along a corridor paved with Minton's tiles and illuminated by ornamental lanterns.[2] In later years, following the demolition of the corridor and removal of the roof and glazing on the footbridge, the 'Glass Bridge,' as it was fondly referred to, became a favourite perch for railway observers and photographers during the final years of steam traction. It was completely demolished in the early 1970's. The original plans allowed for a tunnel to branch off from the subway on the island platform and run under the tracks, with a deep cutting on the other side to accommodate the covered way. This idea, however, was quickly abandoned as it was deemed to be impracticable.

Pen and ink drawing from the London Illustrated News, 1882 *(Author's collection)*

Access from the direction of the town was by way of East Cliff and Vicar's Bridge. Prior to the arrival of the railway in Preston, there was a pathway connecting the fashionable areas of East Cliff and West Cliff, which must have been quite a pleasant and scenic walk in those days and might well have been traversed by Charles Dickens, who visited the town in 1854. When the NU arrived, the path crossed the tracks by way of German's Bridge, which disappeared when additional tracks were laid in the 1870's.

The hotel 's architecture is based on a pleasing mixture of Queen Anne, Elizabethan, Gothic and Renaissance styles; the external walls being built of Welsh Ruabon red brick, with Crosshill stone string courses and red Runcorn dressings. The roofs are covered with red Staffordshire tiles, resembling terracotta. Perhaps the most outstanding feature of this 3-storey building is the lofty tower which has a narrow balcony at the top, bordered by a stone-capped crenellated parapet. The top-most room contained a cold-water feed tank, with a capacity of 2000 gallons. During the last war, the tower was used as a fire-watcher's lookout post and any of the guests who wished to ascend the structure out of curiosity were discouraged by tales of a lady in grey who was reputed to haunt that particular part of the building. It was later disclosed that the story was nothing more than a ruse, conjured up by the servants for the purpose of preventing senior members of the staff from discovering their secret hide-away.

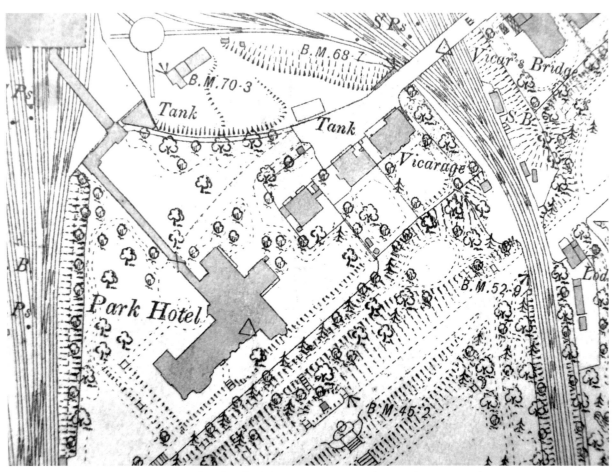

1896 map showing Park Hotel and railway *(Author's collection)*

Main entrance to building *(Author)*

East elevation *(Author)*

The noted Preston historian, Hewitson, said of the building: *'The frontage to the south is 174 feet long, and that to the west 152 feet. Surmounting the general building there is a tower, 113 feet 9 inches in height from base to finial. The external architectural aspect of the hotel is, on the whole, fine, massive, stately, picturesque; but in colour the structure looks too red: age will, however, tone it down considerably in this respect; while familiarity with the building will wear off what at first sight has an incongruous appearance in the higher or surmounting part - the close contiguity of a chimney or ventilating shaft with the tower.'* [3]

It is also of interest to note that in the first variety performance at Mr. Harry Hemfrey's New Gaiety Theatre in Preston in 1882, the drop-scene was embellished with a painting of the 'New Railway Hotel', as observed from Millar Park. [4]

Construction date on west gable *(Author)*

South-West turret *(Author)*

The interior is spacious with wide stone staircases which were originially covered with heavy Axminster carpeting, and the high corridor walls are lined up to a height of 4 ft. with different coloured glazed tiles, forming artistic panels. The area above the tiles is faced with a material known as 'Lincrusta Walton' and the ceilings adorned with ornamental plaster mouldings. The furnishing was supplied by Messrs. Benham & Co., of London and fitted by Maple & Co. of Tottenham Court Road, London; it pertained to a simple but substantial style, easy to clean and not too cumbersome.

The plumbing work was carried out by The Sanitary Engineering Company, of Victoria Street, Westminster. There were special rooms for dining, writing, commercial meetings, smoking and billiards. The original plans allowed for a bar, but this wasn't put in place until much later, alcoholic beverages being drawn from the cellars and served in the dining room or taken to the guest's rooms on request.

There were no fewer than 10 private sitting rooms, each with a couch, easy chairs, an extendable oval table, a writing table, a buffet and a sideboard. The ground floor coffee room measured 42 ft. 6 ins. by 25 ft.; the drawing room, 23 ft. 9 ins. by 26 ft. and the reading room, 18 ft. 6 ins. square. The coffee room was furnished with 18 tables, each having room to sit 4 persons; the flooring here being made of polished pinewood. The drawing room carpets had a parquet margin made of ¼" thick oak, cut out joined and tongued together in geometrical forms.

The accommodation above comprised 33 double bedrooms, 29 single, 6 drawing rooms and, surprisingly, only 8 bathrooms.

There was central heating in the building, but this was confined to the ground floor with the upper rooms having coal fires which had to be kept going in cold weather by staff armed with some 70 coal scuttles. Similarly, although most of the rooms had ablution facilities in the form of wash basins or wash-hand stands, there was no hot water supply, so this had to be delivered in large earthenware jugs, on demand, by the chambermaids.

Looking east from the tower *(Author)*

Chimney detail from tower *(Author)*

The hotel became the property of the LMS railway in 1923, and things remained much the same until 1934 when some long overdue modernisation took place, which included the installation of hot running water and some extra bathrooms at a cost of £3,500. During the war, essential maintenance only was carried out, with the replacement of the laundry boiler and some repair work to the garage roof costing £850. The staff had to work hard for their coppers and were expected to put in a 72 hour week. Jack Saunders worked there as a junior porter in the early 30's: *'Porters earned 19 shillings and 9 pence weekly plus tips, uniform and meals, but the staff meals were much inferior to those of the guests. For example, meal charge for a guest's dog was 2 shillings and sixpence, while the costing for a staff meal was 5 pence. Charge for bed and breakfast was 30 shillings, dinner one pound and five shillings and a pint of beer two shillings and a penny, compared with one penny a pint in the nearby pubs'.* [5]

A surviving bill for June 3, 1903 informs us that the guest in room 6B paid one pound and eighteen shillings for an overnight room, breakfast, luncheon and three glasses of beer.

The sturdy and impressive tower with ventilation stacks on the west side *(Author)*

In July 1888, the train carrying the Prince and Princess of Wales (later to become King Edward V11 and Queen Alexandra), stopped at Preston around midnight on the way back from Scotland, where they had opened the Glasgow Exhibition. The Royal Saloons were shunted into a 'quiet area' within the station so the princess could have a cat-nap before breakfast. I have no idea as to where a quiet area could have existed on such a busy station, unless it was by the horse-dock on the west side. The Princess breakfasted on the train whilst the intrepid Prince and his entourage went up to the Park Hotel for theirs.

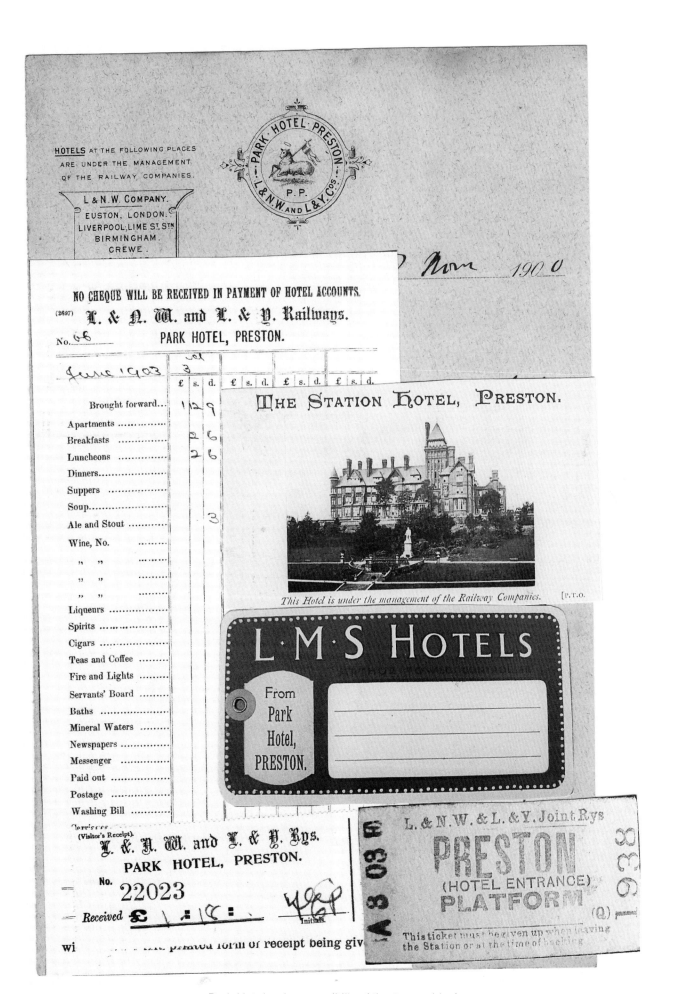

PARK·HOTEL·PRESTON·
P·P·
L & N.W. AND L & Y. Cos.

HOTELS AT THE FOLLOWING PLACES ARE UNDER THE MANAGEMENT OF THE RAILWAY COMPANIES.

L & N.W. COMPANY.
EUSTON, LONDON.
LIVERPOOL, LIME ST. STN.
BIRMINGHAM.
CREWE.

Nov 1900

NO CHEQUE WILL BE RECEIVED IN PAYMENT OF HOTEL ACCOUNTS.
(2697)
L. & N. W. and L. & Y. Railways.
No. 66   PARK HOTEL, PRESTON.

June 1903	3											
	£	s.	d.	£	s.	d.	£	s.	d.	£	s.	d.
Brought forward...	1	2	9									
Apartments		2	6									
Breakfasts		2	6									
Luncheons												
Dinners.................												
Suppers												
Soup.....................												
Ale and Stout			3									
Wine, No.												
,, ,, ...												
,, ,, ...												
,, ,, ...												
Liqueurs												
Spirits												
Cigars												
Teas and Coffee												
Fire and Lights												
Servants' Board												
Baths												
Mineral Waters												
Newspapers												
Messenger												
Paid out												
Postage												
Washing Bill												
Carriages												

The Station Hotel, Preston.

This Hotel is under the management of the Railway Companies.   [P.T.O.

L·M·S HOTELS
From Park Hotel, PRESTON.

(Visitor's Receipt).
L. & N. W. and L. & Y. Rys.
PARK HOTEL, PRESTON.
No. 22023
Received £   Initials.
wi .... printed form of receipt being giv...

L. & N.W. & L. & Y. Joint Rys
A 3 03 V
PRESTON
(HOTEL ENTRANCE)
PLATFORM
(Q)
638
This ticket must be given up when leaving the Station or at the time of booking

Park Hotel ephemera *(Mike Atherton archive)*

Notable visitors to the hotel in the 1930's included Stanley Baldwin, Paul Robeson, Paderewski, Richard Tauber, Gracie Fields, Sir Thomas Beecham, Sir Malcolm Sargent and John McCormack. Some of the wealthier guests made the hotel their long term residence and one such person was Lockhart Marshall, the works manager at English Electric, who lived there for some 30 years up to the hotel's closure. The only significant event to take place in the hotel's 68 years was the Board of Trade enquiry into the derailment of the Scotch Express, which occurred north of Preston in July 1896. The enquiry was chaired by Colonel York.

The building's role as a hotel ceased within two years of nationalisation. British railways took over in 1948 and some 12 months later produced a memorandum which stated that in the year 1937 the hotel had made a profit of £3,363, but by the close of 1948 it had made a loss, which for that year was declared as £4,032. BR had also totted up the cost of bringing the hotel up to date; it needed repairs to the structure, installation of central heating, rewiring and redecorating, new furniture, some additional staff rooms, together with changes to the dining and bar areas. This was quite a list with a suitable price tag of £31,550. By this time (1949), the hotel had 50 letting bedrooms available, the whole of the top floor having been given over to staff accommodation, leaving four floors and a basement. It still remained the biggest and best hotel in the town boasting a large dining hall with a capacity to suit 86 guests, two lounges, a private dining room with 50 seats, four private sitting rooms and a billiards room, with views of and access to Miller Park as a key feature. On November 17, 1949 the Board held a meeting and agreed to sell the hotel. There was a lengthy debate regarding the foot bridge and the access road, and how they would go about maintaining a 'right of way'.

Notwithstanding the fact that the building was on the asset register at £55,216, they had estimated its value at auction around £35,000 to £40,000. The hotel was sold on January 3, 1950 subject to contract, for £85,000, the highest bidder being Lancashire County Council. The second highest bidder was the North Western Electricity Board with £59,000 and in third place was a consortium of Preston businessmen, who declared their bid of £55,000 in the hope of retaining the building as a hotel. This disparity between the bids turned out to be a sore point for Lancashire County Council; however, they eventually negotiated some additional concessions, such as the inclusion of a few chattels, valued at £15,000 and a £710 price reduction together with a waiving of any contribution towards the repair and maintenance of the access road and Vicar's Bridge. Also included in the price was £2000 for the licences required in order to operate as office premises. This left a balance of £67,290 as payment for the actual buildings and, of course, the land. The sale caused a fair amount of press interest and even resulted in local people forwarding letters to their MP's in an effort to retain the building as an hotel for the town, which had few suitable establishments in the area. One local MP, Doctor S. Segal, wrote a letter to the Rt. Hon. Lord Inman PC J.P., chairman of the Hotels Executive at British Railways, stating his concern about the loss of accommodation and its impact upon the town and its prospects for trade.

Although Dr Segal received a sympathetic response, Lord Inman confirmed that having received a firm offer for the hotel, it would not be possible to defer the matter. The sale was finally completed on Monday September 4, 1950 and LCC took vacant possession on the Wednesday. The impressive aspect of this magnificent structure was blighted somewhat in 1963, when a drab, concrete high-rise extension was built in close proximity to the west wing. It was a hideous example of thoughtless planning and incurred the wrath of many people in the town, who rightly referred to it as an outrageous monstrosity.

The Lord Derby statue, which stands in Miller Park by the side of the Broad Walk at the base of the hotel embankment, was unveiled by Colonel Wilson Patten, M.P. on June 3, 1873. According to Hewitson, the ceremony was attended by some 40,000 persons. The statue, weighing 6 tons, is made of white Sicilian marble and is 11 ft. in height. It stands upon a polished grey granite pedestal, 13 ft. 6in. high, which in turn rests upon a grey and red granite base, 3 ft. in thickness, the whole weighing some 40 tons. The inscription reads: 'Edward Geoffrey Stanley, 14th Earl of Derby, K.G. Born 29th March 1799. Died 23rd October, 1869'. On the back of the pedestal is the inscription: 'North and North East Lancashire Derby Memorial, 1873'. The sculptor was Mr M. Noble, of London. The statue occupies the site of the 'Belvedere', an ornate pavilion or summerhouse which was erected there in 1866. This attractive little structure was carefully dismantled and rebuilt on a site to the east of the park, where it stands to this day.

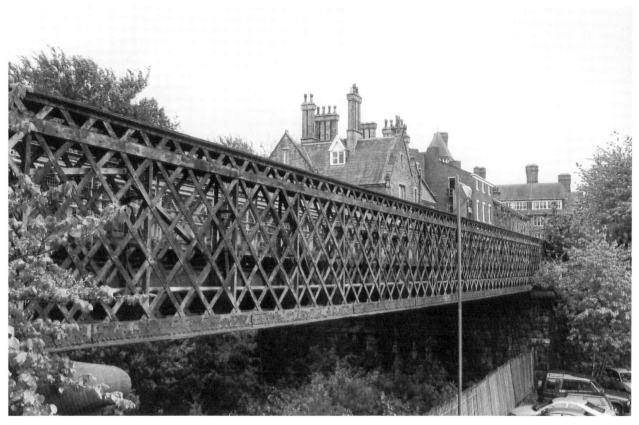

Looking west along the parapet of Vicar's Bridge in recent times.
The first building on the left is the old vicarage. *(Author)*

FOOTNOTES

[1] Thomas German was a flax manufacturer and had a factory in Leighton Street, Preston. He financed the construction of St. Peter's Church and was, for a while, president of the Institution for the Diffusion of Knowledge. In 1832 he purchased an elevated parcel of land and built a mansion on it which he named "The Cliffe," hence the names East and West Cliff. He died on 18th September, 1847. In 1877 his trustee, William Charnley, sold the estate to the joint companies for £7,833.00, the transaction being authorised in accordance with the North Union Railway Act, 1875.

[2] This was the main entrance and was on the north-west side at the rear of the hotel. The door leading from the porch to the reception area is at an angle to the external door, which helps to prevent draughts.

[3] Hewitson, History of Preston

[4] Preston Guardian, September 2, 1882

[5] Lancashire Evening Post, 1982

CHAPTER SIX

The Whitehouse Triangle

The first signal box to be encountered south of the Ribble bridge was Whitehouse North Junction. This was an all timber cabin measuring 23 ft. x 12 ft. with a platform elevation of 7 ft. 6 ins. It had a LYR frame with 26 levers and a locking box and controlled a section of the main line and access to and from the Southport line. In addition to this there was a trailing cross-over, which permitted movements when the triangle was being used for turning locomotives.

Whitehouse South Junction was the next box up the line. This was originally named Whitehouse Junction before the north curve was added in July 1900, to enable trains to travel direct from Southport to Butler Street, by-passing the WLR station. The box was rebuilt as a standard LYR timber cabin in 1920 and measured 20 ft. 6 ins. x 12 ft. with an elevation of 8 ft. 6 ins. and was fitted with a LYR frame of 20 levers and three locking boxes. As with the north box, it controlled the junction and a trailing crossover for engine movements.

Fairburn tank No. 42675 approaches Whitehouse North Junction
with a short off-peak local train to Southport *(Jack Hodgkinson)*

Whitehouse West Junction completed the triangle at a point close to where the Southport line passed beneath the west coast main line. The box had a brick base with wooden superstructure, measuring 20 ft. x 11 ft. with an elevation of 7 ft. 6 ins. It had a LYR frame with 24 levers and two locking boxes.

All the lines in this triangle and the main line out of Preston were operated under absolute block and the speed limit on the curves to Whitehouse West Junction was 20 m.p.h., with the main route from Preston being 40 m.p.h. The triangular formation was useful for turning locomotives and an extract below, from the signal box register of Whitehouse South Junction, shows six turning movements. In all cases, on this particular day, the light engine arrives along the up line from Preston and is crossed over to the down line and sent on to Whitehouse West Junction. Here it is crossed over once more and sent on to Whitehouse North Junction on the down line. Occasionally a light engine arriving from the same direction would be sent to the west junction first, but this would depend on the order and density of traffic.

How Signalled	Is Line Clear Accepted	Train Arrived	Out of Section Signal	Rear or Advance Section	Remarks
2-3	7.56 a.m.	7.58 a.m.	7.59 a.m.	To West	RF*
2-3	7.59 a.m.		8.2 a.m.	Xover	RF*
2-3	12.41 p.m.	12.45 p.m.	12.46 p.m.	To West	RF*
2-3	12.45 p.m.		12.58 p.m.	Xover	RF*
2-3	3.11 p.m.	3.14 p.m.	3.16 p.m.	To West	Turn**
2-3	3.16 p.m.		3.17 p.m.	Xover	Turn**
2-3	3.45 p.m.	3.47 p.m.	3.48 p.m.	To West	Turn**
2-3	3.47 p.m.		3.49 p.m.	Xover	Turn**
2-3	5.7 p.m.	5.11 p.m.	5.14 p.m.	To West	Carnforth?
2-3	5.14 p.m.		5.16 p.m.	Xover	Turn**
2-3	6.16 p.m.	6.19 p.m.	6.20 p.m.	To West	Turn**
2-3	6.19 p.m.		6.22 p.m.	Xover	Turn**

Shaded rows represent the 'Down' page of the register
* Signalman P. Kellet on duty 6.0 a.m. (box opened)
** Signalman T. Stamp on duty 2.0 p.m. (off duty 10.0 p.m. - Box closed)

The table demonstrates the slickness with which these operations were carried out: as the locomotive is signalled and arrives at the box it is offered to Whitehouse West Junction, crossed over and sent on its way. You can see also how different signalmen refer to the operation as 'Turn' or 'RF', which refers to 'round the fork'. Why the comment mentions Carnforth is unclear; perhaps the engine was being prepared for a Carnforth working. The table heading, 'How signalled' refers to the block bell code for a light engine.

Signal box lad's cap badge

Iron bridge on the north junction curve. *(Mike Norris)*

Factory Lane tunnel beneath the East Lancs. tracks at Whitehouse. *(Author)*

Accidents at the Whitehouse junctions

Turning engines proved to be the cause of all the accidents at Whitehouse. The following gives an account of two incidents, both being head on collisions:

Collision September 25, 1920 at 8.10 am. at Whitehouse South Junction, Preston, on the Lancashire & Yorkshire Railway. A Blackburn to Preston down passenger train, headed by 2-4-2 radial tank No. 1157, travelling at considerable speed on the main line under foggy conditions, collided with a six-coupled light engine, No. 625, which was standing on that line. Twelve passengers suffered from shock and various superficial injuries. The driver of the passenger train was, however, seriously injured and the fireman severely shaken. Fortunately neither engine became derailed; locked together they travelled 218 yards. Signalman Fletcher made the initial mistake in placing the light engine on the main line when he thought he had pulled the points for the branch line; however, owing to poor visibility, he could not see the engine and correct his mistake, and was too busy with subsequent trains. It was firmly fixed in his mind that the engine was on the branch line. When the driver of the light engine realised the mistake he sent his fireman (Walker) to the box to advise the signalman, who said *'alright mate, I know'*, but did nothing and just left the box to set detonators for the fog. Fletcher denies Walker gave him the message, otherwise he would still have had time for the shunt. *'It is unlikely that the accident would have happened had track circuits existed; this is a good example of the value of the protection they afford. They were planned for installation but obtaining materials had delayed the process, the installation was completed when I held the inquiry'.* [1]

A Black 5 negotiates the tight south curve between the
south and west junctions, with a train for Southport. *(Alan Castle)*

View from the footplate of a class 2 loco of the North Union bridge and the junction layout at Whitehouse West beyond. The trailing points, which were used for turning locomotives, are located ahead of the junction and controlled by ground signals. *(Alan Castle)*

Collision November 20, 1924 at 7.10 pm, between a passenger train and a light engine at Whitehouse North Junction on the LMS. The 7.08 pm. Preston to Ormskirk passenger train was approaching Whitehouse North Junction on the up line with all signals set for the movement, when it collided with a light engine. The latter had run around the Whitehouse triangle with the object of turning and was travelling back to Preston in a facing direction on the same line (having failed to cross over to the down line). Nine passengers suffered from shock and slight injuries and one of the engine drivers, Robert Banks aged 59, a driver since 1905, was killed. The second driver, Harry Tate aged 41, a driver since 1916, was fatally injured. The two firemen and the guard were also injured.

The passenger train was drawn by 2-4-2 radial tank engine No. 10676 which was running chimney first and had a total weight of 55 tons 19 cwt with an 8 wheeled non corridor 3rd class van No. 2955; an 8 wheeled non corridor composite coach No. 111352 and an 8 wheeled non corridor 3rd class van No. 241. The light engine had left Preston tender leading and had run to Whitehouse West, clearing the points; the disc cleared for the crossover road and it ran chimney first towards Whitehouse South. The home signal came off when it was within 20 yds., it then ran past the Whitehouse South signal box.

B.R. standard pacific, 72007 Clan Mackintosh, approaches the west junction box with a train from Preston to Southport. *(Alan Castle)*

Austerity, 90595 thunders past Whitehouse South Junction with a through freight.
Note the lean on the signal box. *(Initial)*

Class 2MT loco, 78048, of Bank Hall shed passing Vernon's factory at Penwortham with a
Liverpool - Preston train. The gas works are just visible in the background. *(Jack Hodgkinson)*

Fireman Mills (of the light engine) stated that *'his driver habitually used the down home signal as a mark for judging the position of the engine and then ran forward until the whole of the engine had passed by the signal post, situated 11 yds. south of the crossover points'.* It is difficult to do otherwise than credit the fireman's evidence that the engine was well clear of the points.

Signalman Bamber (of Whitehouse South signal box) states that *'he waited until he received a whistle from the engine to indicate it was in its proper position before he pulled over lever No. 9 to work the points of the crossover. He then showed the enginemen a green hand lamp to show they could set back'.* Bamber has 30 years experience and his actions show he was fully alert to the work in hand. Owing to the darkness of the night the signalman could not have told it was running on the up line instead of the down until it was quite close to him and too late to prevent the accident. It is equally difficult to discredit his story. Both cannot be correct otherwise the engine would have moved on to the down line.

Unfortunately past experience of mistakes made by both enginemen and signalmen does not make it possible for me to rule out entirely either alternative as a possible explanation of the failure of the engine to take the crossover road points. I am therefore unable to offer a positive opinion whether the initial responsibility for this accident rests with the enginemen Tate and Mills or with signalman Bamber.

Apart from the initial mistake, responsibility rests upon driver Tate who failed to notice for over a distance of half a mile that he was travelling on the wrong road. Fireman Mills must share responsibility for lack of alertness, being in a better position to judge whether the engine was on the proper road, and his failure to place the leading white light in front of the tender in its proper central position.

'It cannot be denied that the existence of a fixed signal in the 6 ft. way, to control shunting movement over the crossover, would in all probability have prevented this particular accident. It has been contended that a previous accident in 1920 at Whitehouse South Junction in which also the use of the crossover road for a light engine was concerned, would also have been prevented, but the circumstances of that case do not support this. Light engine movements in connection with shunting or turning operations on running roads have been a comparatively fruitful source of accidents in the past, there is need for additional protective measures'. [2]

There was a locomotive turntable at the East Lancs station, but it was not considered to be balanced enough for two men to work a large engine round by hand.

A Fairburn tank eases through the west junction points with a small stopping train for Southport. *(Alan Castle)*

Another shot from the footplate giving a good view of the west junction box, points and south curve. *(Alan Castle)*

FOOTNOTES

[1] Ministry of Transport Railway Accidents, 25th September 1920. A. Mount Major R.E.

[2] Ministry of Transport Railway Accidents, 20th November 1924. J.W. Pringle, Colonel.

CHAPTER SEVEN

The Gas Works at Lostock Hall

Perhaps one of the more prominent features to be observed when travelling on the East Lancs. line between Todd Lane and Preston, was the massive gas producing complex at Lostock Hall. I can recall how the gas holders and buildings seemed to appear of a sudden as the train followed the northward curve away from Todd Lane Junction and the cutting began to level out. Even more imposing was the scene at night, when the towering structures, tubes, valves, chimneys, tracks and tankers were illuminated by a myriad of brilliant lamps, each with a bluish aura. My young and imaginative mind interpreted this striking aspect as a possible rocket site or something out of one of Mr Asimov's books. The quest for the Moon was all the rage in those days.

In 1924, the Preston Gas Company (formerly Preston Gaslight Company, 1815 - 1839) acquired 34 acres of land for the construction of a new works at Lostock Hall, adjoining the west side of the East Lancs line. The production station was divided into two sections, the East and the West Works. The former was the first to be developed, and by 1931 it was capable of producing some 5 million cubic feet per day. The existing production stations in the centre of Preston were subsequently closed down and the work force transferred to Lostock Hall. A larger carbonising plant was added in 1944 and the construction of two carburetted water gas plants in 1949 increased production to 9.25 million cubic feet per day. [1]

The site at Whitehouse prior to construction,
with Penwortham Mill in the background. *(Jim Heron archive)*

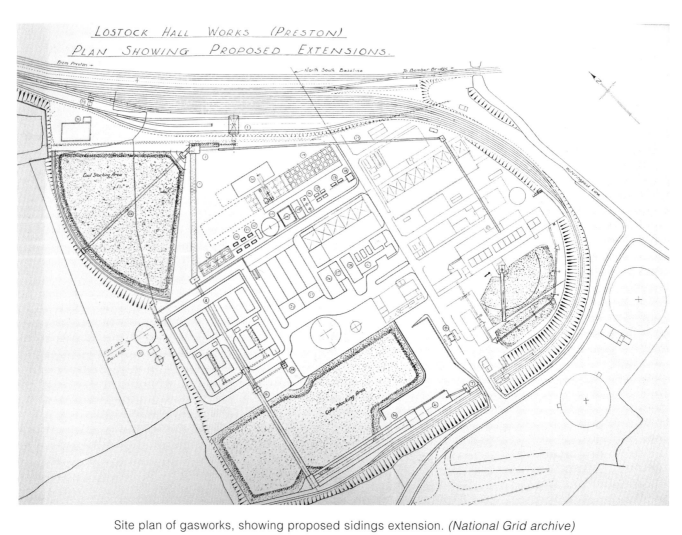

Site plan of gasworks, showing proposed sidings extension. *(National Grid archive)*

One of the gas holders as seen from beneath the road bridge *(Jim Heron archive)*

There were two gas holders at the works, each incorporating a 4-lift, spirally - guided steel tank. Number 1 was built in 1928 and had a capacity of 3 million cubic feet, and number 2, built in 1952, had a capacity of 2 million cubic feet. A large amount of coal was consumed by the steam and power plant, which was equipped with two Lancashire boilers on the ground floor and three waste-heat boilers on a stage floor. All the boilers operated at a pressure of 150 pounds per square inch and were fully adequate for all steam requirements in the works, with two waste-heat boilers and one Lancashire boiler providing an ample supply of steam at all times. The feed water was heated to a temperature of 170 degrees Centigrade by exhaust steam.

The boiler dimensions are as follows:-

No. 1 Waste heat boiler, 9 ft. diameter by 20 ft. long.
No. 2 Waste heat boiler, 8 ft. diameter by 22 ft. long.
No. 3 Waste heat boiler, 8 ft. diameter by 22 ft. long.
No. 4 Lancashire boiler, 9 ft. diameter by 30 ft. long
No. 5 Lancashire boiler, 9 ft. diameter by 30 ft. long.

An odd-looking saddle tank, possibly an American Porter or Baldwin design, which could have belonged to the contractor or have been the first works locomotive. The smaller dome-like covers would have contained sand to prevent the wheels slipping. Note the different couplings and steam whistle. *(Jim Heron archive)*

The brand new rotary wagon tipper *(Jim Heron archive)*

In 1950 it was decided to centralise gas production in the Preston area at Lostock Hall and eventually close down the production stations at Garstang, Leyland and Chorley. A parcel of land with an area of 6.25 acres was purchased to accommodate the new West Works, which comprised an intermittent vertical - chamber carbonising plant with a capacity of 4 million cubic feet per day; coal and coke handling installations, ancillary plant and new sidings. Site clearance commenced on June 10, 1953 and work started on the deeply piled foundations on June 29, 1953.

The new coke screening plant was opened in January 1956 to cope with the peak loads of coke production on the existing vertical retort plant. Additional railway sidings were commissioned in August 1956 and the new tray purifiers put to work with gas from the East Works in October of that year. Gas production on the new I.V.C. plant commenced on November 21 and the gas works at Garstang, Leyland and Chorley were subsequently closed down. The third and final section of the carburetted water gas plant was completed and put into commission on October 1, 1956, giving a gas production of 14 million cubic feet per day, with one C.W. gas plant in reserve as stand-by, having a capacity of 1.5 million cubic feet per day.

Private sidings were constructed adjacent to the main line in 1926 with connections to the up and down lines. Originally they consisted of four tracks, but as the works expanded they were replaced by a 'balloon' pattern arrangement, comprising ten tracks with accommodation for 195 wagons. Following the completion of the West Works, a spur to the new coal-handling plant was built. The works had its own shunting locomotive, a Pecket 0-4-0 saddle tank, number 1820.

Carbonizing plant *(Jim Heron archive)*

View from the north. The old farmhouse looks out of place, and there's
no mistaking who the gas engineers were: Drakes Ltd. of Halifax. *(Jim Heron archive)*

Access to the works was originally controlled by the 'Preston Gas Co. Ground Frame', which was released from Preston Junction signal box. When the sidings were enlarged, they were then controlled directly from the same box using motor operated points (circa 1956).

There were standing regulations for the working of the 'North Western Gas Board's Sidings' – *"When the Gas Board engine is observed to be working in the vicinity of connections which require to be used by the B.R. engine, the guard must obtain assurance from the person in charge of the Gas Board engine that no conflicting movement will be made during the time the B.R. engine is in the sidings." "When the train is ready to leave, the Guard (Fireman in the case of a light engine) must immediately advise the Signalman at Todd Lane Junction (Preston Junction) of the destination and loading of the train, by means of the telephone provided adjacent to the signal controlling the exit there from."* [2]

Finally another ground frame was commissioned on this site with the introduction of the Preston PSB; the line from Lostock Hall Junction being called 'Butler St. Goods Line' or 'Todd Lane Gas Works Siding'. It was worked under 'One train working' regulations.

The single-line staff which *"is kept in a release instrument located adjacent to the Notice boards 480 yards from the junction points at Lostock Hall, lettered Commencement/End of single line, and is released by track circuit occupation. When the train has returned and the staff replaced in the release instrument, the signalman at Preston box should be advised by telephone."* [3]

This section of the line remained in use long after the rest of the 'Preston Extension' had closed, but the siding was closed and taken out of use on November 30, 1977.

Plenty of interesting detail here: the site is being levelled out for the exchange sidings with the help of a locally owned steam shovel. The spoil is being carried away in narrow gauge tipper trucks which appear to be under the charge of an internal combustion locomotive. In the background the main line crosses Leigh Brow, at the top of which, the buildings on the left belong to Leigh Brow Farm, and on the right, Leigh House Farm.
(Jim Heron archive)

Trip workings to the Gas Works Siding

In 1947 inward coal traffic and chemical bi-products from the works were typically serviced twice a day, except Saturday and Sunday when there was only one service. By 1962, this had changed slightly with only one service on Monday and no Sunday service. In all cases these worked from Lostock Hall Sidings with any outgoing goods and empties on to Bamber Bridge.

No. 23 - Class 3 Freight Engine (partial table)					
Trip working between Lostock Hall C&W, Lostock Hall Sidings, Gas Works Sidings, Bamber Bridge, Preston West Lancs and Preston E.L.					
	arr. **MO** a.m.	dep. **MO** a.m.		arr. **MX** a.m.	dep. **MX** a.m.
Lostock Hall Sdgs.	3.25	3.45	Lostock Hall Sdgs.	3.25	3.35
Gas Works Sdgs.	3.55	4.15	Gas Works Sdgs.	3.45	4.5
Bamber Bridge	4.51	5.15 L.E.	Bamber Bridge	4.38	5.5 **MSX**
				arr. **SUN** a.m.	dep. **SUN** a.m.
			Lostock Hall Sdgs.	2.50	3.35
			Gas Works Sdgs.	3.45	4.28
			Bamber Bridge	4.36	4.50 L.E.

Trip workings in and out of Gas Works Sidings June 16 to October 5, 1947

No. 26 - Class 3 Freight Engine (partial table)		
Trip working between Lostock Hall Sidings, Farington Jn. Bamber Bridge, Gas Works Sidings and along the line to Hoghton.		
	arr. **SX** p.m.	dep. **SX** p.m.
Lostock Hall Sdgs.	6.10	6.25
Gas Works Sdgs.	6.35	7.18
Bamber Bridge	7.48	8.0 L.E.

Trip workings in and out of Gas Works Sidings September 10, 1962 until further notice

The last resident loco at the works was this 0-4-0 saddle tank built by Peckett. It carried the maker's number 1820 and was delivered new in 1931. She is seen here with her proud crew in October 1954. *(Frank Smith)*

No. 20 - LOSTOCK HALL TRIP ENGINE Class 8F (Std. 2-8-0)	arr. SX	dep. SX
	p.m.	p.m.
Bamber Bridge	8.55 A	9.25
Lostock Hall Sdgs.	9.33	10.5 L.E.
Lostock Hall Shed	10.10	11.55 L.E.
	a.m. MX	a.m. MX
Lostock Hall Sdgs.	12.0	12.15
Preston E.L.	12.30	12.55
Lostock Hall Sdgs.	1.10	1.30
Ribble Sidings	1.48	2.30
Kirkham	3.1	3.58
Bamber Bridge	4.40	
	a.m. MSX	a.m. MSX
Bamber Bridge		4.55 B
Lostock Hall Sdgs.	5.0	5.20
Gas Works Sdgs.	5.32	6.15
Bamber Bridge	6.25	6.45 L.E.
Lostock Hall Shed	6.50	
	a.m. SO	a.m. SO
Bamber Bridge*		5.55
Lostock Hall Sdgs.	6.0	6.22 C

* Shunt Goods Yard and as required (work from Bamber Bridge).
A - After working 7.57 p.m. From Southport.
B - Convey Lancaster Traffic.
C - Work 6.22 a.m. To Southport

No. 23 - LOSTOCK HALL TRIP ENGINE Class 8F (Std. 2-8-0)	arr. SO	dep. SO		arr. SUN	dep. SUN
	p.m.	p.m.		a.m.	a.m.
Lostock Hall Shed		7.55 L.E.	Preston N.U. Yard	12.5	12.30
Lostock Hall Sdgs.	7.40	7.55	Lostock Hall Sdgs.	12.45	1.0
Preston E.L.	8.7	8.38	Bamber Bridge	1.5	1.30
Lostock Hall	8.53	9.5	Lostock Hall Sdgs.	1.35	2.40 L.E.
Gas Works Sdgs.	9.16	10.15	Lostock Hall Shed	2.45	
Bamber Bridge	10.25	10.50			
Lostock Hall Sdgs.	10.55	11.16 A			
		a.m.			

FOOTNOTES

[1] Visit to Preston north Western Gas Works. Chairman's day July 3, 1954. Institute of Gas Engineers. (National Grid Archive)

[2] Sectional Appendix Central Lines, October 1, 1960. British Railways.

[3] Sectional Appendix Northern Section, November 1963. British Railways

CHAPTER EIGHT

Lostock Hall

LOSTOCK HALL

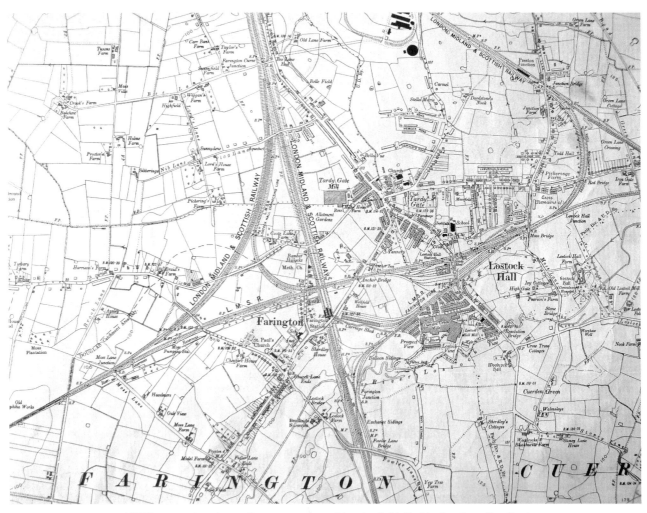

1930's map showing railway complex at Lostock Hall. *(Author's collection)*

The arrival of the Blackburn and Liverpool lines at Lostock Hall in 1846 gave prominence to this small rural town. A railway community was established which was to last for 122 years, with one in ten of the town's men folk being employed on the railway around the turn of the century. A station, goods shed and sidings were built on the east side of Watkin Lane bridge, and some time later the LYR built extensive carriage & wagon repair shops on the west side of Moss Lane bridge.

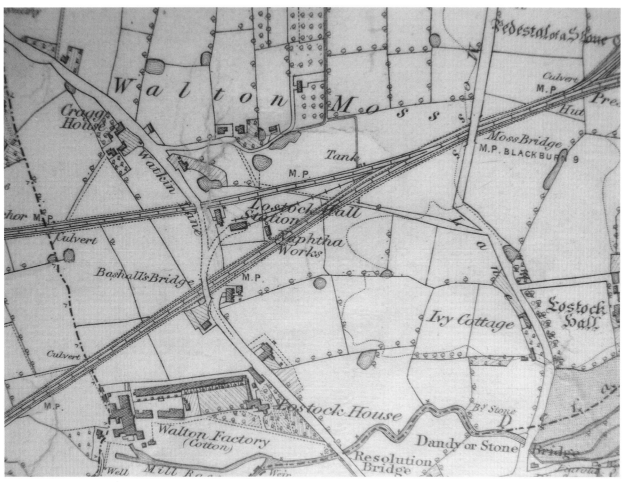

Early map showing the original station at Lostock Hall. *(Author's collection)*

Postcard showing Lostock Hall station in LYR days. *(Sommerfield Collection)*

A new station was built on the west side of Watkin Lane bridge in 1883. The buildings were constructed of timber throughout, in the traditional LYR style, with the emphasis on structural economy, using 9 ins. x 1 ¼ ins. rusticated pine boarding on 6 ins. x 6 ins. timber frames, with red brick chimney stacks and slated roofs.

The booking office was adjacent to the south end of the road bridge, the platform being accessed by way of a flight of timber steps with half-way landing. A lamp room was located between the underside of these steps and the bridge abutment. The building measured 30 ft. x 15 ft. with a height of 12 ft. from floor joists to ceiling, and comprised a narrow booking hall with double doors at each end, a booking clerk's office and an office for the station master at the rear. Members of staff in 1883 included Robert Carter, station master, James Iddon, booking office clerk and William Moss, porter. The station master's house was on Moss Lane, just round the corner off Watkin Lane.

The waiting rooms on either platform were identical in outward appearance, measuring 36 ft. x 12 ft. with a height of 10 ft. 6 ins, and the ladies waiting room incorporated a wash room, partitioned off to 13ft. 6 ins. The only significant changes which took place in the station's lifetime of 86 years were the removal of the gentlemen's lavatory block on the up platform and it's replacement with a brick structure on the down platform, and the installation of two small cabins for staff and storage facilities at the foot of the booking office staircase.

The station and shed from Watkin Lane
in the 1960's *(Initial)*

Station booking office from Watkin Lane,
7th October 1964. *(R.J. Essery)*

There were eight cast-iron lamp columns on the up platform with seven on the down, and these, together with the smaller parapet columns at the top of the staircase, were originally fitted with pendant globes. The LMS replaced them with lantern type tops, and these in turn were replaced in the late 40's by the standard 'Sugg' pattern with pendant globes and copper shades. As with so many other stations, gas lighting was used right up to the end. The station was closed on August 7th, 1968 amid uproar from local people, and it wasn't until some 16 years later, in 1984, that BR responded favourably to campaigners and opened a new station on the east side of Watkin Lane bridge, which was virtually on the site of the original ELR building.

The goods shed, with its distinctive ELR design, was located on the east side of Watkin Lane bridge, adjacent to the exchange sidings. It was served by a single straight-through track, which originally terminated at a wagon turntable, connecting it with a siding on the north side and a short coal siding running 90 degrees to the south side of the shed. The walls, which measured 52 ft. x 32 ft. with a height of 20 ft. to the underside of the roof-trussing, comprised random rubble sandstone trimmed with ashlar coping and rusticated quoins and voussoirs. The gabled, slated roof had originally been built with sky-lights, but these were removed in later years. The vertical timber-framed windows with fanlight tops, of which there were two on the south side and three on the north, measured 8 ft. x 3 ft. The interior was furnished with a timber loading platform, jib hoist and sliding door; and a slated canopy, following the pitch of the main roof, protected the loading area on the south side. Tell-tale signs on the west wall indicated the existence of a long removed small, gabled building, possibly a former weigh office. A staff of 6 men (per shift) would have worked in the goods and coal yards, which were under the charge of the station master. The main carting agents in 1898 for the LYR in that area were Hopwood Bros. The sorting sidings comprised 10 roads, a cattle dock, two shunter's cabins and a yard crane. When a particularly lengthy train was being back-shunted, and the locomotive was east of Moss bridge and round the corner, the driver, unable to see the ground signal, would have had to be called on by means of a powerful klaxon horn, which was located somewhere near the goods shed.

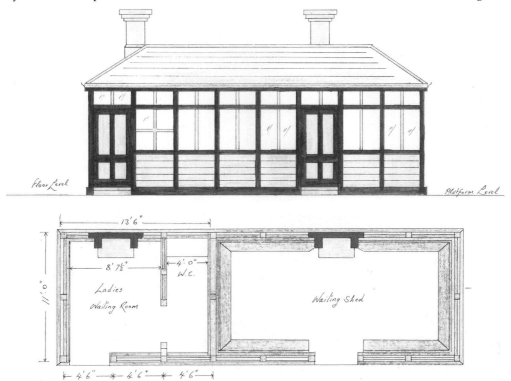

Plan & elevation of waiting room. *(Drawings by author, taken from measurement of buildings in 1969)*

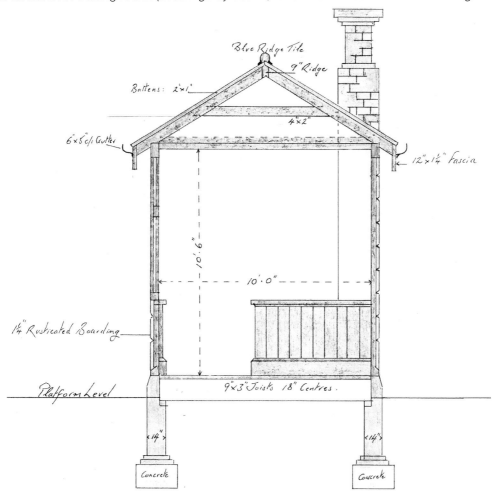

Waiting room, side elevation

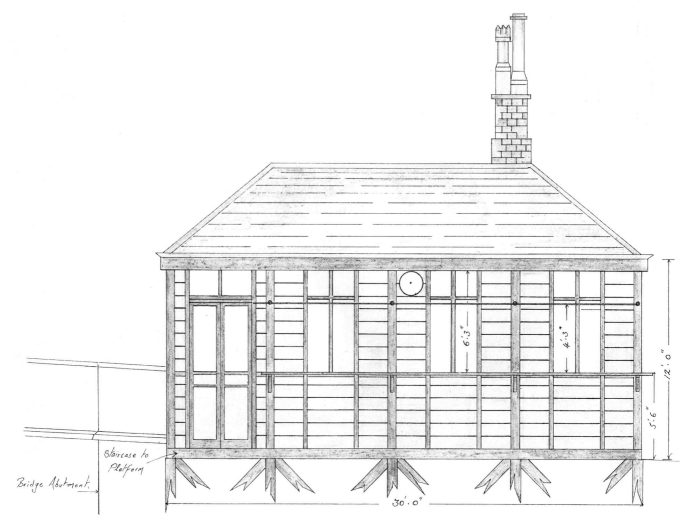

Booking office, west elevation

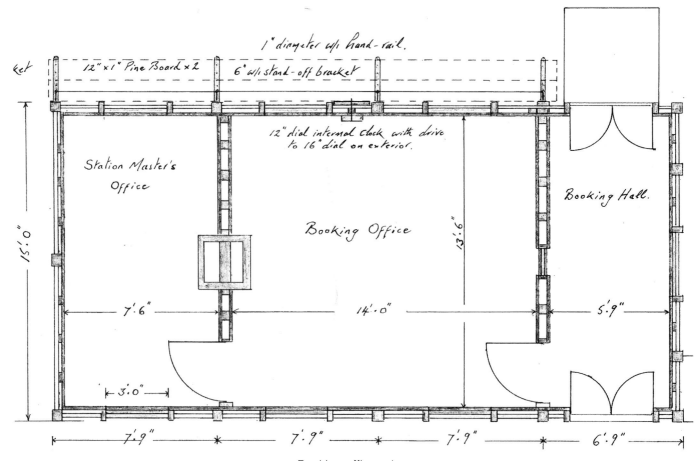

Booking office, plan

Newton Heath Jubilee, 45601 British Guiana, at the station with an express
for Liverpool Exchange, via Moss Lane Junction and Ormskirk. *(Chris Spring)*

Everything stops for a few moments at Lostock Hall sorting sidings, while the photographer secures for
posterity the portrait of an immaculate engine, No. 66, her crew, the yard foreman and a couple of shunters in
the early 20th century. *(David Hunt)*

Goods shed & sorting sidings

Facilities for the yard staff came in the form of a LYR open air brick toilet block, located between the north side of the goods shed and the down main line, close to the original site of the station signal box. Each shunter's cabin was equipped with a solid fuel stove, upon which the eggs, bacon, bangers and toms were cooked in a blackened iron frying pan. Water for the 'char' was boiled in a large cast-iron kettle, which was kept topped-up and simmering throughout the working day.

These time-honoured and traditional methods continued long after the 1950's washroom and canteen facilities had been built across the way, between the re-located station box and C&W shops. The goods shed closed in the early 1960's and the coal yard and sorting sidings closed in 1968.

Lostock Hall goods shed on May 29, 1965.
Of interest is the coal merchant's sack-rack in the foreground. *(Noel Coates)*

The carriage & wagon shops were built on the west side of Moss Lane bridge (now named Todd Lane South). It was a timber plank and frame structure on a brick base and was some 200 ft. in length with two through roads. It was extended somewhat by the LYR in 1900, with additional sidings to the north, and a small single track shed near the bridge which served as a workshop for private-owner wagons. The site was closed down and operations transferred to the redundant engine shed in 1971. Demolition followed shortly after.

With less than a month to go before the end of steam and the closure of the sorting sidings at Lostock Hall,
45287 shunts an assorted rake of wagons on 19th July 1968.
The timber carriage and wagon shops are on the right. *(Initial)*

The massive carriage shed at Lostock Hall was built in the mid 1880's. It measured 660 ft. in length by 41 ft. 6 ins. in width and 17 ft. 4 ins. from the top of the rails to the underside of the tie beams. It contained three roads with 6 sidings on the north-east side of the building, and such was its length that the north-west end terminated within a few yards of Croston Road bridge, adjacent to Farington station. The shed was built entirely of timber, with the regulatory 3 ft. 6 ins. space between the ground and bottom horizontal frames on each side. The glazed gabled roof was built up with king-post trussing and supported internally by a row of timber columns either side of the centre road. The walls and gable screens at each end comprised vertical tongue & grooved boarding and the entrance at the south-east end had two sets of three folding doors. Each road had inspection pits and drains, the pits being paved with blue engineering bricks-on-end. Most isolated railway buildings had their own tips and this was no exception: a large crater adjacent to the sidings was filled in over the years with old beer bottles, damaged crockery and tobacco fallout. At around the same time as the carriage shed was being constructed, a connection was put in between the back line and the engine shed at Lostock Hall. This was to save time when sending engines to the south of Farington and vice versa. A wrought-iron latticed footbridge was built to replace a level crossing on the back line, which was part of a public right of way from Ward Street to Croston Road.

The Royal train, or Blue train as it was referred to, was kept here and was run regularly to Horwich and back when not in official use, as a precaution against seizing up. One retired railwayman chuckled as he recalled the Horwich run:

'Folks used to gather by the line side and on bridges along the way, trying to catch a glimpse of the monarchy. The only person they saw was his majesty the guard glowering at them from the brake.'

Some of the Coronation Scot carriages were also stored here for a short while following their withdrawal in 1939. Some years later a number of vintage carriages, covered in tarpaulins, were kept in store until accommodation could be found for them at York Museum. The shed was used mainly for the storage, cleaning and light maintenance of excursion and relief stock, carriages for the ROF workers train and the 'Croston Bus'. Another story, this time relating to the latter train was told by ex-Lostock Hall driver, Andy Hall:

'The fireman on the Ormskirk train had lost his shovel in the firebox, and the driver had phoned the engine shed asking for a replacement. The foreman handed a shovel to one of the cleaners and told him to give it to the driver of the Croston Bus. The young lad, who was a bit new to the job, set off to the bus stop near the Pleasant Retreat pub in the village, where he tried to hand it over to the man in charge of a machine with four wheels instead of 12. The Corporation bus driver sent him on his way and the lad returned to the shed amid roars of laughter. He soon learned the true identity of the Croston Bus and when he arrived at the train, the driver asked him if he'd been to Preston to get the shovel.'

There were some spectacular stock movements to be seen here in the 1960's. Lostock Hall fireman, Jim Marlor recalls an empty stock trip from there on Royal Scot class loco, 46118, with driver Pete Norris, piloted by a class 5 with driver Jack Dean and fireman Jack Brady, to Carlisle with 20 carriages. They didn't require a banker at Tebay, but one came up behind them just in case.

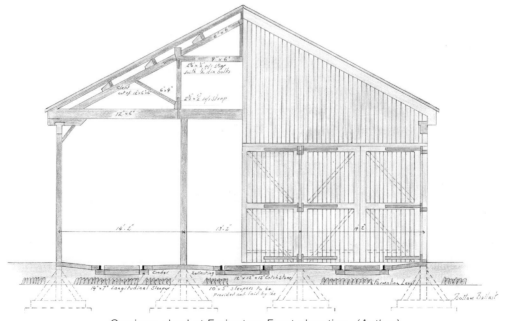

Carriage shed at Farington, Front elevation. *(Author)*

The Railway Hotel off Watkin Lane was a convenient establishment for the railwaymen, and for many years the Ward family brewed and bottled their own beer at the back of the premises. *(Leyland Library)*

The well kept bowling green and pavilion at the rear of the Railway Hotel. The News of the World bowling finals took place here in 1954, with the winner collecting a £200.00 cash prize.
Note the back line signals peeping over the pavilion roof. *(Leyland Library)*

West Along the Line

Leaving Bamber Bridge or Preston Junction, the first signal box along this section of line was Lostock Hall Junction. This RSCo signal box of 1886 had a brick base and timber superstructure; it replaced an earlier cabin which was on the other side of Moss Lane, nearer the junction itself, on land later used as a head shunt. The new 40 lever RSCo. box was built against the retaining wall on the north west side of Moss bridge, adjacent to the carriage & wagon works. It measured 25 ft. 1 ins. x 12 ft. and was so constructed as to provide the signalman with visibility over the road bridge. It controlled the junction with Bamber Bridge and Preston Junction, the junction to the back line towards Lostock Hall Carriage Sidings and Lostock Hall Station. It also controlled access to Lostock Hall up and down sidings.

Ex-Lostock Hall and Crewe driver, Bert Stewart, mentioned this box as having a connection with a certain passing-out ceremony:

'The passed cleaner was encouraged to stand beneath the open smoke vent on the cab roof, minus his cap, as the engine approached the box; the driver then gave an easily recognisable series of short blasts on the steam whistle, in return for which, the signalman tipped a bucketful of soiled water onto the cab and, being well practiced in the operation, a good quantity of the sordid contents found its way through the hole and soaked the unsuspecting candidate.'

The working of vehicles on running lines without a brake van in the rear (Rule 153) was authorised between Lostock Hall Junction and Farington Junction, on both up and down lines (60 wagons). The movement of coaching vehicles without brake van in rear was also authorized between Lostock Hall and Preston E.L. Goods, limited to 4 vehicles.

The lofty signal box at Lostock Hall Junction. *(Author's collection)*

A ground frame had also been installed in 1886 to control the down sidings and access to the goods warehouse. It was called Lostock Hall Junction Ground Frame and consisted of 12 levers; it was located in the 'V' between the back line and lines to Lostock Hall station. Next along the back line was Lostock Hall Carriage Sidings, this was an RSCo. cabin of 12 levers with a brick base and timber superstructure. It controlled access to the carriage sidings, the engine shed spur and the line to the LNWR cabin at Farington Junction. This section was worked Permissive Block (except for passenger trains), with a speed limit of 25 m.p.h.

Lostock Hall Carriage Sidings box. Note the ladder against the fence
which facilitated a shortcut to the Railway Hotel. *(Tom Wray)*

Moving back to Lostock Hall Junction and following the lines westwards, the next cabin is Lostock Hall Station. There have been two signal boxes on this site, the original one being on the south side of the line, adjacent to the goods shed, and the second on the north side. This was a LMS all-timber design with a 30 lever Railway Executive Committee (REC) frame of 1946/7. It controlled access to the up and down sidings (the up sidings also contained the Carriage and Wagon works). It should be noted that during the mechanical period the up direction is towards East Lancashire and the down direction towards Ormskirk. The box was located on the north side of the line close to the site of the original station.

Trip workings in and out of Lostock Hall Sidings
June 16 to October 5, 1947

Although a few freights arrived and departed directly from Lostock Hall sidings most of the freight traffic was worked by the local trips.

No. 22 - LOSTOCK HALL SHUNT Class 2 Freight Tank Engine					
1.30 a.m. MO to 6.0 a.m. Sunday					
	arr. **MO**	dep. **MO**		arr. **SUN**	dep. **SUN**
	a.m.	a.m.		a.m.	a.m.
Lostock Hall Shed		1.30 L.E.	Lostock Hall Sdgs.		5.55 L.E.
Lostock Hall Sdgs.	1.35		Lostock Hall Shed	6.0	
Trips as required to Farington Junction					
Engine to Shed for Coal 7.30 a.m. to 8.30 a.m. **MX**					
Engine to Shed for Coal 5.30 p.m. to 6.30 a.m. **Daily**					

No. 23 - Class 3 Freight Engine					
	arr. **MO**	dep. **MO**		arr. **MX**	dep. **MX**
	a.m.	a.m.		a.m.	a.m.
Lostock Hall Shed		1.15 L.E.	Lostock Hall Shed		1.15 L.E.
L'ock Hall C&W.	1.20	3.20	L'ock Hall C&W.	1.20	3.20
Lostock Hall Sdgs.	3.25	3.45	Lostock Hall Sdgs.	3.25	3.35
Gas Works Sdgs.	3.55	4.15	Gas Works Sdgs.	3.45	4.5
Bamber Bridge	4.51	5.15 L.E.	Bamber Bridge	4.38	5.0 **MSX** L.E.
Lostock Hall Sdgs.	5.25	6.50	Lostock Hall Shed	5.5	
Preston W.L. Yard	7.15	8.10 E&B	Bamber Bridge		5.5 **SO** L.E.
Lostock Hall Shed	8.28		Lostock Hall Sdgs.	5.10 **A**	

Where freight trains terminated at Lostock Hall, guards were required to place their 'Goods Guards Reports (E.R.O. 48216)' in the box provided in the Guards room, instead of handing them to the drivers. [1]

In 1918 an accident in the goods yard came to the attention of the railway inspectorate, acting on behalf of the board of trade. The National Union of Railwaymen were also involved, and asked if they could arrange for a representative to be present on their behalf, as two railway employees, guard A. Parkinson and shunter W. H. Cornell, were cited in the report.

The accident occurred on March 15, 1918 at 7.45 am. and appertains to a knee injury to one John Fazackerley, employee of a local coal merchant, who was working on business at the time. The accident book report reads:

'Whilst standing on the door of a wagon supported by a prop, filling bags of coal, some vehicles which were being shunted, came into contact with the wagon causing him to fall to the ground. The usual notice prohibiting the propping of wagon-doors is prominently exhibited in the yard & the wagons were "closed-up" in the ordinary way; it is stated however that the shunter did not attend to the brakes, & also he should have seen that all was clear before the shunting was commenced'. The reason for this accident was given as *'Due to his own misconduct and the negligence of another person'.*

The Lancashire and Yorkshire Railway response to the railway inspectorate's findings was that *'the company has no power to compel outside firms to discontinue the practice of propping up wagon doors, every effort is made to impress upon them the desirability of doing so'.*

Clearly this practice continued well into modern times. Many later photographs of coal yards show this as a fairly widespread activity.

An evocative picture of the interior of Moss Lane Junction box at night. The signalman poses on the blower by the light of an oil lamp. Note the Midland pattern signal lever frame. *(Jeff Mimnagh)*

	arr. **SUN**	dep. **SUN**		arr. **SUN**	dep. **SUN**
	a.m.	a.m.		a.m.	a.m.
Lostock Hall Shed		12.30 L.E.	Gas Works	3.45	4.28
L'ock Hall C&W	12.35	1.40	Bamber Bridge	4.36	4.50 L.E.
Lostock Hall Sdgs.	1.45	2.0	Lostock Hall Sdgs.	4.55	5.10
Preston E.L.	2.15	2.40 E&B	Bamber Bridge	5.16	5.30 L.E.
Lostock Hall Sdgs.	2.50	3.35	Lostock Hall Shed	5.35	

A - On SO works 6.25 a.m. To Southport

No. 27 - Class 3 Freight Engine

After working 6.22 p.m. Burscough Bridge to Lostock Hall Sidings

	arr.	dep.		arr.	dep.
	p.m.	p.m.		p.m.	a.m.
Lostock Hall Sdgs.	7.8	7.37	Bamber Bridge	10.34 **A**	3.35
Bamber Bridge	7.42 **A**	9.25 L.E.		a.m.	
Preston (Butler St.)	9.32	20.23	Lostock Hall Shed	3.40	

A - Loco. Duties

No. 28 - Class 3 Freight Engine

After working 9.52 p.m. Aintree Sorting Sidings to Lostock Hall Sidings

	arr. **MX***	dep. **MX***		arr. **MX***	dep. **MX***
	p.m.	p.m.		a.m.	a.m.
Lostock Hall Sdgs.		11.0 L.E.	Lostock Hall Sdgs.		2.50
		a.m.	Maudlands	3.11	3.20 L.E.
Preston (Butler St.)	11.15	12.30	Lostock Hall Sdgs.	3.36 **A**	6.50
	a.m.		Preston W.L.	7.15	8.10 L.E.
Lostock Hall Sdgs.	12.42	1.15	Lostock Hall Shed	8.30	
Ribble Sidings	1.35	1.50 L.E.			
Lostock Hall Sdgs.	2.0				

* Not shown in actual document as MX but is shown in WWT as such (assumes a print error)

A - Loco. Duties

Other Trip Workings (full details shown elsewhere)

No.	From	arr.	dep.	To
15	Farington Jn.	12.6 a.m. **MX**	12.35 a.m. **MX**	Maudlands
15	Farington Jn.	8.15 p.m. **SO**	8.15 p.m. **SO**	Maudlands
24	Farington Jn.	5.5 a.m. **MO**	5.30 a.m. **MO**	Bamber Bridge
24	Bamber Bridge	7.33 a.m. **MO**	7.45 a.m. **MO**	Farington Jn.
24	Farington Jn.	9.5 a.m. **MO**	9.25 a.m. **MO**	Bamber Bridge
24	Lostock Hall Shed	3.5 a.m. L.E. **MX**	3.20 a.m. **MX**	Farington Jn.
24	Farington Jn.	4.15 a.m. L.E. **MX**	4.55 a.m. **MX**	Bamber Bridge
24	Bamber Bridge	7.55 a.m. **MX**	8.20 a.m. **MX**	Farington Jn.
24	Farington Jn.	9.5 a.m. **MX**	9.25 a.m. **MX**	Bamber Bridge
25	Lostock Hall Shed	6.5 a.m. L.E. **SX**	11.10 a.m. **A SX**	Preston (Butler St.)
25	Preston W.L.	1.7 p.m. **SX**	1.20 p.m. L.E. **SX**	Lostock Hall Shed

An unidentifiable Super D passing the shed with a train of perishables for Liverpool. *(Jack Hodgkinson)*

Further West

The next signal box along this section of line was Lostock Hall Engine Shed. The original box of 1882 was located directly opposite the exit from the then new engine shed on the east side of Croston Road (originally called Farington Lane).

The new box, a LYR timber cabin of 40 levers, was approved by the board of trade on October 10, 1907. This box was located on the west side of Croston Road and controlled access to the engine shed and the new connection to Farington Curve Junction. Continuing west, the next box was Moss Lane Junction. The original 1889 structure was a RSCo. cabin with a 23 lever frame, being replaced in the mid-thirties by a standard LMS box containing a 20 lever frame. This controlled the junction from Ormskirk, north to Farington Curve Junction and Preston or east to Lostock Hall and completed the south westerly triangle. The junction arrangement also included a trailing crossover as with the Whitehouse boxes, but there is no evidence this was used regularly for turning locomotives.

A Church procession on Croston Road in the early 20th century.
Lostock Hall Engine Shed Box is prominent in the background. *(Leyland Library)*

The engine shed box looking east, in the LYR era. *(David Hunt)*

As the line from Farington Curve Junction to Lostock Hall Engine Shed was on a climb of 1 in 78 the sectional appendix states:

'Assisting engine to leave the train at Lostock Hall Engine Shed box. To avoid unfitted freight trains from running away on the gradient there is a warning board, 280 yds. past the engine shed box, advising drivers to stop and apply wagon brakes, which are not to be released until the train reaches Ribble Sidings.'

Also noted in the 1969 sectional appendix for Lostock Hall:

'Drivers requiring to leave the locomotive sidings must advise the signalman by telephone of the number of the train they are going to work.' (3)

The line from Lostock Hall Junction through to Lostock Hall Engine Shed climbed slightly, on an average gradient of 1 in 655, levelling out to 1 in 2106 as it passed the engine shed box. Apart from where stated, all main lines were subject to absolute block working.

Today the lines from Bamber Bridge follow the same alignments as the original routes, except that the route from Lostock Hall Junction to Farington Junction (back line) has been straightened and overhead 25KV catenaries added, leading to the raising of the metal foot bridge in Ward Street, although most of the original structure survives to the present time. Following the commissioning of the Preston PSB scheme (1972), two sidings were added to allow electric locomotives to be changed for onward Diesel traction, but never really saw their intended purpose, although they were used a number of times for steam specials and are still extant. Two loops were proposed off the back line with the intention of forming a freightliner depot but the plan was never implemented.

A Lanky 0-6-0 travelling tender first towards Farington, as seen from the iron footbridge. The carriage sidings are on the immediate left and the engine shed is visible in the background. *(D. J. Tomlinson)*

Rebuilt Patriot, 45521 Rhyl, passes the carriage shed with passenger stock for the Royal Ordnance Factory at Euxton. *(Stan Withers)*

Along the main line towards Farington Curve Junction, a loop for the sidings of the former carriage and wagon works (north side of the line) was proposed, but again, not put into effect. Access to the former engine shed (south side of the line) was maintained and had the name 'Lostock Hall Depot' which remained in use until the building closed.

With the introduction of the Preston PSB the line to Moss Lane Junction was also removed on May 1, 1972, the only access being directly to Farington Curve Junction. All lines are signalled from Preston PSB using Track Circuit Block (TCB), except for the back line from Farington junction to Lostock Hall junction which is permissive block for freight trains. It is interesting to note that the naming of the lines in the power box was reversed from mechanical days: the 'Up East Lancs' lines are now in the Preston direction and the 'Down East Lancs' lines are in the Blackburn direction.

FOOTNOTES

[1] General Appendix to the working time tables with sectional appendix. Central Division, March 1937. LMS.

[2] British Railways.

[3] Sectional Appendix to working time tables 'Northern Section' June 1969. LMR. British Railways.

8F 48081 drifts through Lostock Hall station with a long train of empties. *(Stan Withers)*

CHAPTER NINE

The engine shed at Lostock Hall

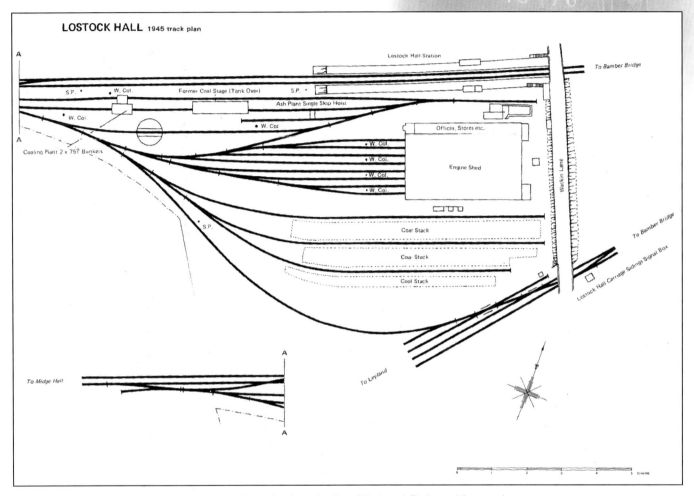

LOSTOCK HALL 1945 track plan

1945 engine shed track plan *(National Railway Museum)*

In 1879, the LYR began looking for a site on which to build a substantial engine shed, as the old 5 road shed at Butler Street was not big enough to cope with the increasing volume of traffic and had been considerably reduced in size and efficiency following the expansion of the Fishergate station in 1877; added to this, the arrangement with the LNWR for sharing their depot at Preston was continually fraught with the usual arguments and conflicts. A decision had to be made, and after some time spent measuring up areas to the south of Preston, the surveyors recommended a site at Lostock Hall, to the west of Watkin Lane, where there were also plans for a new station.

The contract was awarded to Bridges & Co. of Burscough, and after much levelling and excavation work, the construction of the new buildings was commenced in June 1881. The work was completed in May 1882 at a cost of £30,000 after a delay of nearly six months, owing to severe weather conditions.

The building which measured 221 ft. in length by 139 ft. in width, was a typical 'Lanky' design, accommodating eight terminal roads with inspection pits and 12 hydrants for boiler-washing and general cleaning purposes. The building incorporated a 20ft. wide block of offices and workshops on the north side, comprising, in order of appearance, from west to east, the shed-master's office with its characteristic bay window façade; a general office for accounts, rosters, wages etc.; a narrow walk-through pay lobby; a mess room for the enginemen; a large storage room with double doors at each side for locomotive tools, oil and lamps; a copper and tinsmith's shop; a smithy, complete with forge and anvil; a narrow storage room for locomotive components; a large room for the fitter's workshop with a timber lean-to office and, finally, the fitter's mess room.

The pay lobby had a sloping desk-top, above which was a small window, opening into the general office. This is where the men submitted their individually numbered brass pay-tokens, in exchange for small tins (each with a corresponding number painted on the top) which contained their weekly wages. The pay tin was generally regarded as being the lightest thing on the railway. The copper and tinsmith's shop became an ambulance room in the late 1930's. The last coppersmith to work there was Bill Miller and the last blacksmith as such, was Tom Glazebrooke.

These men were quite versatile: when they weren't fashioning parts for the engines, they would busy themselves making and repairing lamps, oil cans and special tools etc. It was interesting to note that in 1968 the locomotive fitters were still using one or two examples of 19th century machinery in the workshop, such as hand-wheel operated vertical borers etc. Most of this antiquated machinery was still there in the 1980's.

LYR eight-coupled goods engine, 1619, on shed around the time of the grouping in 1923. She was given the number 12939 by the LMS. *(Frank Dean)*

Ex-LYR 4-6-4 Baltic tank, 11116, in early LMS days. *(Frank Dean)*

The roof had 13 transverse gables of the north light pattern, each with an equal pitch of 30 degrees, as opposed to the conventional 90 degrees scalene pattern. It was supported by 24 wall corbels and 36 cast-iron tubular columns which also served as rainwater down-spouts. Smoke was extracted from the building by way of timber ducting and roof vents, of which there were 96 in total.

The washroom facilities (for want of a more appropriate appellation) came in the form of a roofless block, located in the south-east corner of the shed. It measured some 30 ft. by 12 ft. and contained 8 W.C 's, one of which was the Shed Master's exclusive box with its own lock and key. The 'Bogs', as they were commonly known, were protected from the elements by sandstone flags, and during the Winter months they became cold, dark, damp and draughty places. Across from these was a large earthenware urinal slab with 6 stalls and a cold water tap in the corner; a flimsy corrugated asbestos canopy above, did little to prevent rainwater dripping down the back of an unwary visitor's neck. As with the collieries, wash basins with hot water, soap and clean towels appear to have been introduced at a much later date, and the few ladies who worked there over the years must have been obliged to use the station facilities across the way.

The yard layout included a tank-over coaling stage with adjacent disposal pits; a Cowans Sheldon (improved pattern) 30 ft. manually-operated turntable and sand-drying facilities. The tank measured 106 ft. x 20ft. with a depth of 3ft. 6 ins. and held 80,000 gallons of water. A sand-drying and storage shed was located at the end of the single track between the engine shed and station. This track was also used for the delivery of supplies to the stores, shunting of coal trucks and for locomotives using the coaling stage and disposal pits. On the south side of the shed there was a large boiler house and bunkers for scrap metal and fire-bricks. There were also three sidings here (roads 9,10 and 11), which ran the full length of the shed. The siding closest to the wall (road 9) was used for the storage of locomotives and empty coal trucks; the original hand-operated breakdown crane and tool vans having also been kept here in the early years. The spaces between these three roads were timbered-over longitudinally with pine boards and old sleepers, which provided a substantial base for the huge coal stacks. These were built up with large cobs of coal on the outside in 'dry stone wall' fashion and filled in with smaller cobs, to an average height of 12 ft. during the summer months, when the bulk purchase of coal direct from the collieries was cheaper. Throughout the hard times of the 1920's, the top course of each stack would be whitewashed in order to deter pilferage. As time went on, the coal had to be shovelled back into wagons, which were then shunted across the yard to the coaling stage.

An amusing anecdote from the 1950's explains how this hefty task was made somewhat easier. It was a common thing in those days for passed cleaners to spend some time labouring in the yard, as they could earn more money there than on the footplate.

One of the best paid jobs involved working on a tonnage rate, by shovelling coal from the stacks into 16 ton wagons. On one or two occasions, however, the graft side of the equation was considerably reduced by way of the plank and strut method.

This was achieved by placing planks lengthways on vertical timber struts inside the truck, leaving a free-board of around two feet. This area was then filled up with coal and the truck sent on its way to the coaling plant. All best-laid plans come off the rails sooner or later, and the labour-saving device was discovered one day, when one of the coal hoppers ceased to function owing to a tangle of broken planks. An inspector came round and noticed that the axle springs on some of the 'full' wagons were not showing signs of being subject to any great weight. Form 1's were issued and the graft element returned to 100%.

Class 3F, 12171 at rest alongside Fowler 4MT tank, 2386, on May 14, 1939.
(R.J. Buckley / Initial Photographics)

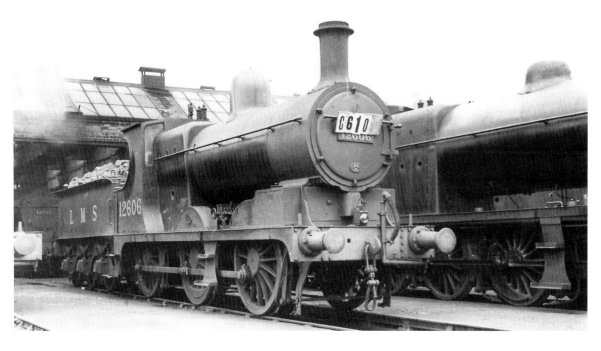

Class 3F, 12606, on a visit. from Accrington shed on May 14, 1939. *(R.J. Buckley / Initial Photographics)*

The open-ended coaling stage had a timber platform upon which coal was deposited from the trucks within. The coal was then shovelled 'up-hill' from the platform into the loco tenders and bunkers through two large bays in the north wall. This laborious task was carried out by a team of six men and, during particularly busy times, cleaners and firemen had to wire in to keep things moving. The large tank above supplied 5 cast-iron water columns, or siphons of the LYR 'elephant head' pattern, of which 4 were located in line about 50 ft. to the west of the shed entrance, each one serving 2 of the 8 roads. They were illuminated by a row of 5 gas lanterns on 12 ft. cast iron columns, set back from the siphons some 15 ft. to the west and spaced such that each lamp stood between two siphons, with one at either end. The 5th siphon stood next to the down main line, adjacent to the site of the future mechanical coaling plant. The shed's water supply was pumped from Farington Lodge, and it is interesting to note that minnows, and other forms of pond life were to be seen swimming around in freshly-filled tenders and tanks.

A train of spare tenders being filled up at Lostock Hall before being taken on to Blackpool Central shed, where there was a water shortage during the Summer of 1911. *(National Railway Museum)*.

The shed was ceremoniously opened on Saturday, June 3, 1882, and the locomotive department officials took possession of the building on the following Monday. The ceremony began at 2.30 pm. at the East Lancs. shed in Preston, where three locomotives had been specially prepared and handsomely decked with flags for the occasion: No 713 Juno, No 695, Cromwell and an unidentified loco, stated to be *'One of the very powerful goods engines, recently added to the company's stock of locomotives'*. (1)

Juno took the lead, with driver John Bullfield on the footplate, one of the company's longest serving enginemen with 40 years service. *'Immediately on leaving the station, what may be termed a 'feu de joie' was fired off by the engines, 21 fog signals having been placed on the rails, and on reaching the bridge over the Ribble, a similar series was discovered to have been placed, as was the case further along the line at Preston Junction.'* (2)

On arrival at the Lostock Hall locomotive siding, Juno was detached and ran forward over the points and then reversed into the shed yard and onto the turntable. After being turned satisfactorily by driver Bullfield and his fireman, the engine entered the new shed amid a fusillade of fog signals and cheers from officials, dignitaries, railwaymen and construction workers alike. A select company was then shown round the building by Mr. Dawson, foreman of the locomotive department at Preston; and afterwards they adjourned to the shed-master's office, where cakes and wine were served. Among those present were three men from the company's head office in Manchester: Mr. McKay, assistant locomotive engineer; Mr. Smith, chief clerk of the locomotive department and Mr. England from the treasurer's office. Others present included, Mr. Bridge, contractor from Burscough Junction; Mr. Billington, proprietor of the Victoria Hotel in Preston; Mr. Crompton, the company's goods agent at Preston; Mr. Edington, waterworks engineer from Lostock; Mr Lusk, the company's clerk of works; Mr. William Thomas, general foreman and other officials from the construction company.

There were a few speeches and toasts, with no record of anyone having had to be carried back to the train. *'Mr Bridge rose to propose the health of Mr. Lusk, who had acted, during the erection of the building, as clerk of works on behalf of the railway company. He remarked that this was the first engine shed that he had had the opportunity of erecting and that he would be very glad to build another.'* (laughter). (3)

Perhaps the most poignant and prophetic speech of the day came from Mr. Dawson, who was to commence work at the new shed on the following Monday as Locomotive Department Foreman. 'He had served over 26 years with the company in Preston, and during that time he had seen many changes, including the development of the station at Butler Street and, indeed, the rapid growth of Preston itself. He went on to praise the attributes of the shed, stating that he had never seen a better planned layout anywhere and that the offices and workshops were the finest on the LYR. There was room for improvement, of course, and that the next shed to be constructed for the company would certainly contain many innovations, but he was sure that in the past, none had been built to equal the new shed at Lostock Hall. (applause)

He then made mention of the last Preston Guild, and recalled the traffic at that time as being 'something extraordinary' and with reference to the arrangements that were being made by the town for the Guild in September, he conjectured that it was going to be 'a great deal heavier than on the former occasion.' He was of the opinion that the Guild of 1882 would wholly transcend all the previous Guilds of Preston, and that it would tax the best energies of the railway company. He went on to say that the company could not begin to make arrangements soon enough for that occasion, for the traffic would be enormous and he was sure it would require all the efforts of the various departments of the company to meet the demands that would be made upon them. (applause)

Also present at the gathering was 63 year old retired engine driver, Jim Redford, of 21 Sackville Street, Burnley. He had brought along his photographic equipment, but sadly the overall dullness of the weather did not permit of any pictures to be taken, and he was obliged to remain seated in a comfortable chair, owing to pain he was suffering as a result of an accident on the railway some 10 months before.(4) With the speeches and toasts over, all present stood up and joined together in a song, thus harmoniously concluding a joyous occasion.

The train returned to Preston by the same route and the engines were stabled at the East Lancs shed, possibly for the last time before their allocation to Lostock Hall. They were to be joined there later on by other former ELR locos, No 630, Phaeton, No 649, Gazelle and No 653, Vivid.

Access to the shed from Watkin Lane was by way of a 'wicket gate', this being the moving part of a small brick building situated a few yards to the south of the station booking office. It was also referred to as the 'Top Lodge' and had a walk-through passage with a booking on/off desk to one side and a brick staircase, with half-way landing, leading down to the shed. The shed's water and gas meters were kept here in the basement. Some years later, an access road to the shed from Watkin Lane was made on the short level stretch between the two bridges.

The Top Lodge was demolished in April 1965 when a banana lorry went out of control on Watkin Lane and ploughed into it. A Reliant three-wheeler which had been parked directly beneath the building was completely crushed and, as the accident had occurred on April Fool's day, the owner of the vehicle, Colin Shaw, who was in the mess room at the time having a mug of tea, refused to believe the young lad who bore the bad tidings. Colin pointed to the date at the top of his newspaper and told him he couldn't be fooled by that one and that when he had finished his brew he was going to thump him round the shed for his cheek. He soon realised the gravity of the situation when a Constable appeared on the scene.

The shed became LYR number 27 and had an initial allocation of some 50 locomotives which, for the most part, comprised 2-4-2 radial tanks, 0-6-0 Barton Wright and Aspinall designs and the Hughes eight-coupled heavy freight locos. For over eight decades the main duties were confined to goods, shunting and local passenger services. The freight routes were mainly Liverpool, Wigan, West Yorkshire and Carlisle, with local pick-up duties including the Burscough and Longridge shunts. For many years the Barton Wright saddle tanks carried out shunting turns at Lostock Hall sorting sidings, Bamber Bridge exchange sidings and Butler Street goods yard. Similarly, the ubiquitous radial tanks dominated local passenger trains on the Preston to Colne, Blackpool, Liverpool, Southport and Longridge lines.

52182 in BR days, showing an area of cab detail. The ex-LYR class 3F's were powerful and reliable engines, but the cabs left much to be desired: there was little room for swinging the shovel, and no seating as such, just an iron splasher box on either side, upon which the crew had to sit side-saddle making sure beforehand that an old sack had been placed between themselves and the cold iron. The cab offered little protection from the elements, and although there was provision for a tarpaulin to be set between the cab roof and a frame at the front of the tender, it had little effect against wind-driven rain in exposed places, as the wet stuff came in at one side and out at the other. *(Author's collection)*

The following is a list of railway staff residing at Lostock Hall in 1898 *(Barrett's Directory)*.

Engine drivers:
John Atkinson, 58 Watkin Lane.
John Barnes, 10 Wilkinson Street.
Richard Baxter, 12 Sephton Street.
John Bradley, 48 Watkin Lane.
Richard Craven, 7 Fairfield Street.
George R Dawson, 18 Watkin Lane.
William Dawson 21 Black Lane. (what is now Brownedge Road)
John Fenny, Lindley Street.
Roland Fish, 9 Fairfield Street.
John W Garside, 4 Wilkinson Street.
Reuben Hale, 19 Black Street.
Joseph Hunt, Tardy Gate.
James Kirkby, 3 Victoria Street.
Charles Lee, 8 South View.
George T Smith, Lindley Street.
William Southworth, 109 Watkin Lane.
James Thompson, 5 Sephton Street.

Firemen:
Simeon Blackwell, 4 Sephton Street.
John Gibson, 87 Watkin Lane.
Thomas H Kirkby, 8 Sephton Street.
Reuben Pemberton, Lindley Street.
Robert Wiseman, Lindley Street.

Guards:
Harry Alston, 17 Black Lane.
William Bendworth, Lindley Street.
Joe Finch, 115 Watkin Lane.
William Hall, Moss Street.
William Holden, 15 Fairfield Street.
Sidney Thorpe, Dilworth Street.
Thomas Tomlinson, 5 Sephton Street.

The driver of Radial tank 10823 is applying a dose of thick green oil to the valve gear while his
mate is busy getting the fire going and ready for the road, on 14th May 1945.
(R.J. Buckley / Initial Photographics)

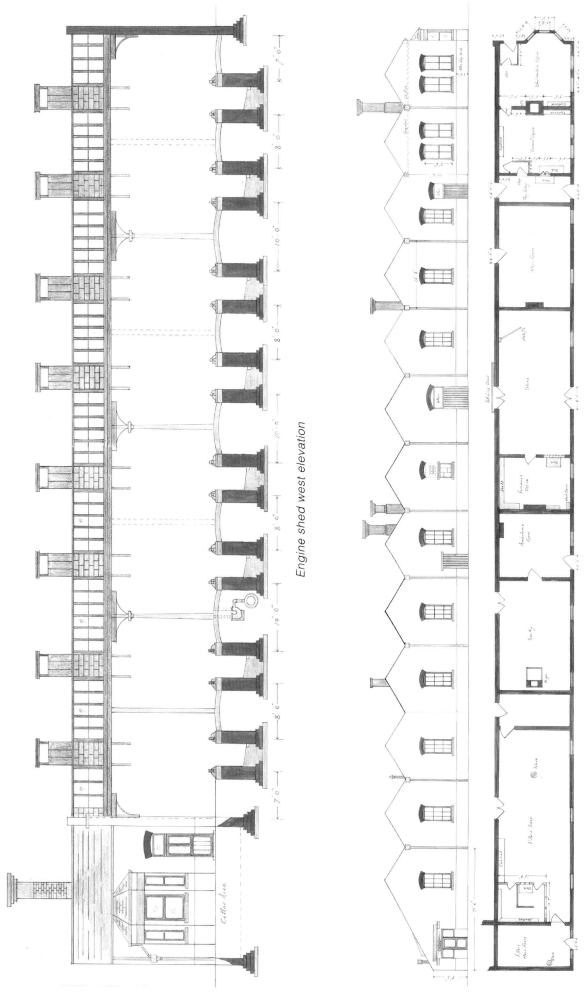

Engine shed west elevation

Engine shed: north plan and elevation. Scale of original drawing: 4mm to 1 ft.
(Drawings by author, from measurements taken in 1989)

Engine No.	Wheel arrangement	Hughes 1920 classification	Year built	Shed No.	Shed name	LMS No.	Withdrawn	Shed on Dec. 31st 1947
			LOSTOCK M.P.D. LOCOMOTIVE ALLOCATION 1922					
16	2-4-2T	5	1892	27	Lostock Hall	10678	Dec-53	Southport
21	0-6-0	27	1893	27	Lostock Hall	12610	Jan-36	
25	0-6-0	27	1895	27	Lostock Hall	12277	Nov-33	
34	2-4-2T	5	1898	27	Lostock Hall	10823	Dec-48	Bury
46	2-4-2T	5	1893	27	Lostock Hall	10687	Sep-53	Southport
55	0-6-0	27	1906	27	Lostock Hall	12436	Feb-46	
82	0-6-0	27	1893	27	Lostock Hall	12209	Nov-32	
121	0-6-0	27	1894	27	Lostock Hall	12222	May-33	
165	0-6-0ST	23	1878	27	Lostock Hall	11348	Sep-53	Bolton
232	0-6-0	27	1894	27	Lostock Hall	12270	Jan-61	Birkenhead
236	0-6-0ST	23	1878	27	Lostock Hall	11345	Oct-56	Lostock Hall
270	0-6-0	27	1894	27	Lostock Hall	12271	Aug-61	Southport
274	0-6-0	27	1901	27	Lostock Hall	12422	Mar-48	Low Moor
321	2-4-2T	5	1892	27	Lostock Hall	10664	Feb-47	
329	2-4-2T	5	1896	27	Lostock Hall	10740	Apr-34	
362	2-4-2T	5	1896	27	Lostock Hall	10741	Apr-37	
365	0-6-0	27	1895	27	Lostock Hall	12299	Sep-54	Bacup
376	0-6-0	28	1901	27	Lostock Hall	12572	Aug-53	Blackpool
472	0-6-0	27	1895	27	Lostock Hall	12308	Aug-34	
479	0-6-0	27	1897	27	Lostock Hall	12362	Nov-52	Aintree
500	0-8-0	31	1900	27	Lostock Hall	[12974]	May-27	
526	0-6-0	27	1900	27	Lostock Hall	12399	Apr-58	Lostock Hall
583	0-6-0ST	23	1881	27	Lostock Hall	11423	Dec-58	Lostock Hall
605	0-6-0	27	1901	27	Lostock Hall	12431	Nov-59	Lower Darwen
668	2-4-2T	5	1899	27	Lostock Hall	10845	Jul-36	
671	2-4-2T	5	1899	27	Lostock Hall	10847	Dec-47	
675	2-4-2T	5	1899	27	Lostock Hall	10850	Oct-61	Mirfield
691	0-6-0	28	1912	27	Lostock Hall	12538	Oct-46	
696	2-4-2T	5	1898	27	Lostock Hall	10809	Jun-46	
759	0-6-0ST	23	1881	27	Lostock Hall	11403	Feb-36	
765	0-6-0ST	23	1881	27	Lostock Hall	11469	May-49	Speke Junction
847	0-6-0ST	23	1885	27	Lostock Hall	11477	Aug-55	Fleetwood
852	0-6-0ST	23	1885	27	Lostock Hall	11491	Mar-57	Sutton Oak
918	0-6-0	28	1912	27	Lostock Hall	12543	Jan-37	
935	0-6-0	25	1887	27	Lostock Hall	12022	Sep-50	Springs Branch
1016	2-4-2T	5	1889	27	Lostock Hall	10629	Aug-38	
1046	2-4-2T	5	1890	27	Lostock Hall	10643	Oct-58	Barrow
1055	0-6-0	28	1890	27	Lostock Hall	12562	Feb-47	
1067	0-6-0	27	1890	27	Lostock Hall	12108	Oct-59	Royston
1113	0-6-0	27	1891	27	Lostock Hall	12132	Mar-57	Newton Heath
1119	0-6-0	27	1891	27	Lostock Hall	12137	Jun-54	Agecroft
1124	0-6-0	27	1891	27	Lostock Hall	12141	Apr-60	Nuneaton
1130	0-6-0	27	1892	27	Lostock Hall	12147	Nov-33	
1142	0-6-0	27	1892	27	Lostock Hall	12155	Dec-47	
1212	2-4-2T	5	1893	27	Lostock Hall	10697	May-52	Bolton
1256	0-6-0	27	1894	27	Lostock Hall	12252	Nov-60	Royston
1280	0-6-0	27	1895	27	Lostock Hall	12289	Oct-59	Lower Darwen
1304	0-6-0	27	1896	27	Lostock Hall	12570	Jun-35	
1340	2-4-2T	5	1897	27	Lostock Hall	10773	Sep-30	
1346	2-4-2T	5	1897	27	Lostock Hall	10779	Jul-37	
1376	2-4-2T	5	1898	27	Lostock Hall	10793	Feb-50	Preston
1463	2-4-2T	5	1905	27	Lostock Hall	10881	Jun-46	
1471	0-8-0	30	1907	27	Lostock Hall	[12761]	Sep-26	
1478	0-8-0	30	1907	27	Lostock Hall	[12768]	Sep-26	
1493	0-6-0	30	1909	27	Lostock Hall	[12463]	May-48	Lostock Hall

The first small batch of ex-Midland locomotives arrived shortly after the grouping in 1923 and comprised 4F, 0-6-0 's, and 3F, 0-6-0 tanks which were, generally speaking, not very popular with the ex-LYR enginemen. The old adage, *'Once a Lanky man, always a Lanky man'* came into effect and they made no secret about their dislike for these 'foreign' engines, the less because they were from a different stable and the more because they had the driver's controls on the right-hand side. Indeed, there were instances where drivers refused to take them out of the shed yard, claiming the engines to be a liability on a system which was effectively rigged-up for them to be stationed on the left-hand side of the cab. Like it or not, they had to live with it until the LMS introduced their own locomotives, based on the MR designs, in 1924.

A later generation of footplatemen spoke quite favourably of the LMS 4F, 0-6-0 's, 3F, 0-6-0 'Jinty' tanks, 4P, 4-4-0 three-cylinder compounds and 4-4-0 two-cylinder light passenger engines, the latter two classes being referred to as 'Long leggers' by the Lancashire enginemen. An old Accrington driver told me that managing a compound correctly was a skill on its own, and that a driver with little or no experience of these engines was hardly likely to get the best out of them.

The sole surviving 4P, number 1000, spent some time at Lostock Hall shed back in the 1940's. Many changes took place at Lostock Hall shed during the 1930's; the first year of that decade saw the arrival of two new classes of locomotive, the Hughes-Fowler 5F (later designated 5MT) 2-6-0 and the Fowler 7F, 0-8-0 heavy freight engine. The former were nicknamed 'Land Crabs' owing to the movement of their large, inclined valve gear, and in later years they were referred to by Lanky men as 'Mae Wests', because of their huge 21 inch cylinders. The latter were fondly referred to as 'Austin 7's' and 'Roasters', owing to the close proximity of the tender to the cab. As with the Baby Austin 7 car, which came out in 1922, the loco was somewhat confined at the business end. Another possible explanation for the hot sobriquet is the fact that, for some reason, these engines had no insulation or casing round their boilers. They were brought in to replace the ageing LYR Hughes designs, which were all scheduled to be withdrawn by the end of that decade. A motive power shortage at the beginning of the war, however, earned them a reprieve and a few of them remained in service until 1948.

Lostock Hall 2-4-2 tank, 10646, at Grimsargh on May 31, 1930. This was the last day of passenger services on the Longridge line, and Driver Billington is shaking hands with the station master, Harold Lathom. *(Courtesy, David. J. Hindle)*

In 1935 Lostock Hall became a sub-shed of Bank Hall in Liverpool, and the shed code was subsequently changed to 23E. Two years later, in accordance with the plans laid down by Mr. E.J.H. Lemon, Vice President for Railway Traffic Operating and Commercial Departments, a reinforced concrete No.2 coaling plant with two 75 ton hoppers was constructed, together with a new Cowans Sheldon 60 foot vacuum operated turntable. The work was carried out by Henry Lees & Co. Engineers, of Glasgow. A steel-framed mechanical ash plant was erected at the same time by R. Dempster & Sons Ltd. [5] The coaling plant towered above the rooftops at a height of 71 ft. 6 ins. and had a lifting capacity of 8 to 20 tons; at the same time, a LMS crane type water column was installed between the turntable road and the ash wagon siding.

The coal road became the engine road and vice versa, and an iron capstan was set in place just a few yards to the east of the coaler, between the coal road and down main line, to enable the trucks to be hauled carefully by rope onto the wagon-lifting platform. This capstan was still in situ in 2008. In 1939, two vertical oil tanks were erected between the old and new coaling plants and a brick boiler-house with pump built onto the south side of the tank-over coaling plant. This was part of an experiment to find out if fuel efficiency could be improved by mixing oil with coal; it soon proved to have the opposite effect, and the idea was abandoned; the tanks, however, remained in situ throughout the war in case a coal shortage necessitated the use of oil. The boiler house was later used for the storage of disposal equipment, and the conical concrete bases for the tanks were still there long after the shed was demolished in 1990.

Ada Ashworth: Bacon Butty Wagon

In 1944, catering facilities were set up at Lostock Hall to provide for the growing number of male and female staff employed at the locomotive and carriage sheds. An eight-wheeled ex-LYR wooden carriage body (possibly one of the vehicles belonging to the old breakdown train) was acquired and cut into two equal sections, which were located side by side between the shed offices and station platform. One section was used for storage and food preparation and the other was fitted out with an oven, sink, hot water cisterns, display shelves and a serving counter.

It was always referred to by the railway workers as the 'bacon butty wagon', and continued to provide refreshments up to the early 1950's. Mrs. Ada Ashworth of Lostock Hall was one of the ladies who worked there. This is a brief account of her early life and her time at the engine shed:

Ada came from a railway family in Preston, and her grandfather had been a shunter at Preston East Lancs, where he lost an arm after being trapped between the platform and a moving train. Notwithstanding this, he went on to become a successful 'one-armed bowler' for his local cricket club. The family moved to Lostock Hall in 1912, where her father worked as a goods guard.

By 1924 he was doing a lot of distance work and spending much time in the 'barracks' at Wakefield. She had seven brothers and one sister; two of the brothers, Howard and Frank, became signalmen. The family was able to travel places further afield once her father had received his privilege pass, and the return fare to Southport was one shilling for her mother and sixpence for each child. Because of the size of the family, her parents took turns in taking half the number to one place and the other half elsewhere at a later date. Ada recalls the huge amount of washing there had to be done each week, and one distinctive item which stood out from the rest on the washing line: her father's red triangular muffler for work, which doubled as a sling in case of an accident. Sadly, her father died on October 2, 1940 aged 56 years. He was suffering from cancer following an accident, when a shunting pole slipped during a coupling operation and struck him in the face.

Tragically, Ada became a war widow in 1944 and was left with two young children to bring up. She was offered a job at the shed in 1945 by the canteen supervisor, Mrs Floyd, a large, homely Irish lady. Thankful for this offer, Ada immediately became a member of staff. The ladies worked in three shifts: early, 06.00 to 14.00, day, 08.00 to 16.00 and late, 14.00 to 22.00; these being worked on alternate weeks with the cook supervisors always on the day shift. When Mrs Floyd retired, Ada took over as supervisor. She fondly recalled her time at the shed:

'They were hard days, and the ingredients were always in short supply, but somehow the staff at the canteen persevered and nobody got left out at meal times. A lot of women worked at the carriage sheds and some of the prettier ones used to get a lift up to the canteen on the footplate. One particularly attractive young lady was called Rose Grove - a name that was to become synonymous with the final months of steam traction. There were the inevitable romances and two of the ladies married men from the shed. Fireman, Harry Moulding, took his fiancé to the cinema one evening. He was late home from work and hadn't time to change into his 'civvies', so he

had to go along as he was, in dungarees and cromby jacket. The film was a typical 1930's 'weepy', which bored Harry to death and caused his fiancé to shed a few tears.

On noticing this, Harry played the gentleman by handing her what he thought to be his hanky. When the film was finally over and the lights came on, the poor girl's face was all smudged with oil and grime. The 'hanky' had turned out to be one of his oil rags which he used on the footplate. There was plenty of laughter and good clean fun, but never any bad language in the presence of the ladies. Mr Turner, the shed master had his dinner sent in to his office each day. A lady called Doreen Counsell worked in his office and three other ladies, Mona Thorpe, Agnes Haythornthwaite and a Mrs Wilding worked in the shed with the men, and all the women had men folk working on the railway. Edith Counsell married Fred Parker; Theresa Molyneaux married Harry Moulding and Doreen Counsell married Mr. Ford.

Everyone enjoyed the bacon and egg butties for breakfast and the favourite mid-day dish for the lads was college pudding and white custard sauce, which was normally only available with a full dinner. The younger lads who could not afford such a luxury would come round later on to see if there were any left-overs.

With free grub in mind, there was no shortage of volunteers to run errands to the village shop and they were always rewarded with a cake and a cup of tea for their efforts. One day, when preparing to make parkin, she sent a young lad to the shop for some oatmeal; he caused a bit of a commotion amongst the staff when he returned with a bag of bone meal.

One of the remaining Hughes 0-8-0 goods engines, 52822, in the yard adjacent to the ash disposal plant. The two halves of the bacon butty wagon are just discernable in the background between the Shedmaster's office and tender. *(Jack Hodgkinson)*

Grand National day was always a busy time for the ladies. Hundreds of people would arrive at Lostock Hall station from East Lancashire and wait there for the Liverpool train. There were many policemen on duty at the station and they used to call down to the canteen for refreshments. Although the facilities were strictly for railway employees only, the staff stretched a point and sent tray-loads of cuppas to the grateful Bobbies. These extra sales helped to boost the coffers and kept the canteen going.'

When the canteen closed in the 50's, one of the coach bodies was removed from the site and the other relocated (by way of steam crane) to the other side of the shed, between roads 8 and 9, in front of the new sand building where it served as a storage shed. Its association with refreshments, however, continued as it became a favourite place for members of the shed staff to have their lunch breaks, albeit on the running board and when the weather permitted.

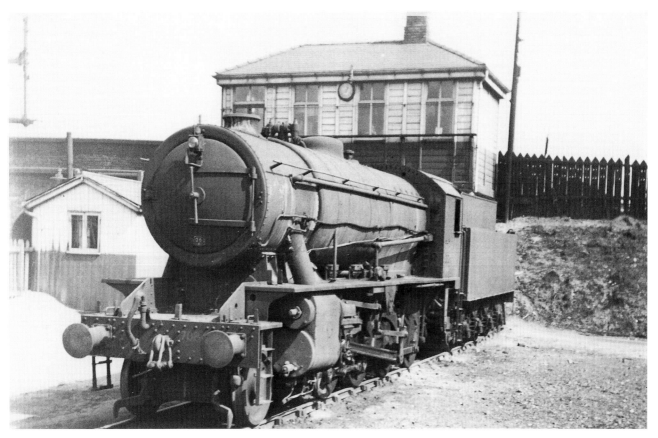

This Austerity 2-8-0 had just arrived from the Western Region, minus her top-feed cover and bearing her old number, 70843, on the buffer beam in 1951. She was later renumbered 90372.
(J. Davenport / Initial Photographics)

The locomotive allocation increased during the war years and train crews found themselves working longer distances and hours. Many of them were away from home for a week or two at a time, putting up in 'barracks' and struggling to find their way along the unfamiliar metals of the Southern and Great Western railways amid blackouts and air raids. Some of the men were temporarily transferred to other depots in the south, namely Nuneaton and Willesden.

Bill Wilson, a former driver, was born in 1917. He started work as a cleaner at Lostock Hall in 1935 and was transferred to Preston in 1945, returning to Lostock Hall as a driver in 1960. He recalled an incident which took place on the 'Long drag' during the Winter of 1940, when the train got stuck in a snow drift at Ribblehead:

'We were low on water and a long way off the water column at Blea Moor, so I had to shovel snow into the tender tank. The weight of snow brought the telegraph cables down, so we dropped the fire and made our way down to the Station pub, where we could thaw out and take some refreshments. We continued taking refreshments for the next two days, because that's how long it took for the snow plough to get through. We were a bit reluctant to leave that place'.

Lostock Hall goods guard, Bill Pollard, recalled a runaway train incident in 1941. The locomotive was another class 7F hauling a munitions train of some 60 wagons from the ROF at Chorley to Carlisle.

'We were routed by way of Blackburn and Hellifield. The engine took water at Blackburn, then we set off up the bank to Wilpshire. We had just got past the summit when things started to get out of control; the wagons jolted and began pushing the engine down the gradient. I knew what was going on straight away, without the driver sounding the S.O.S on his steam whistle. We had a runaway train to deal with. I clambered from one wagon to the next until I got three of them with their brakes pinned down. Sparks were cascading upwards from the wheels and lighting up the night sky, and the noise was terrific. I suddenly became aware that we were crossing Whalley viaduct many times faster than the maximum speed limit of 5 miles per hour - I found out later that we had actually been doing 80 . Anything could have happened: the viaduct might have collapsed or the train might have blown up, taking Whalley with it. We eventually came to rest somewhere between Whalley and Clitheroe and, after examining the train for any damage, I gave the all clear to continue the journey. That's the way it was in those days.'

Lostock Hall montage, comprising: paperwork, tickets, brass pay tokens and small images.
(Author's collection. Photos: Bill Ashcroft)

In 1946, the Fowler 7F's began to thin out in the wake of newly de-mobbed Austerity 8F 2-8-0's. These were powerful engines and well liked by the drivers; the firemen had a different opinion, however, owing to an incurable shudder on the tender which resulted in coal showering forward onto the footplate. The unwieldy eight-wheeled tenders also had a tendency to end up on the floor when negotiating tight curves and points. More taper boiler types began to appear on the shed and the once numerous radial tanks, some of which had already been superseded by Fowler class 3, 2-6-2 and 4P, 2-6-4 tanks, dwindled further in the wake of Stanier 4MT, 2-6-4 tanks. The shed code changed again in 1946 to 24C, when Lostock Hall was placed under the auspices of Accrington (24A). More Stanier 8F, 2-8-0's and Black 5's were allocated to the shed, further reducing the number of pre-grouping locomotives. British Railways took over in 1948 and apart from the introduction of Fairburn 4MT, 2-6-4 tanks, no significant changes took place until 1953, when the shed was given a new roof. This work had been scheduled to go ahead in 1947 by the LMS, but the looming prospect of nationalisation caused it to be shelved indefinitely.

Stalwart Fairburn tank No. 42297 at rest alongside Jinty tank No. 47472, referred to as 'City of Preston' by staff and enthusiasts alike, owing to the number of times she was rostered on the Preston Station Pilot duty; indeed, she had the title painted on her tanks at one time. The gaffers at Preston Control, however, didn't think too much of the idea. *(Peter Ditchfield)*

LOSTOCK HALL M.P.D. LOCOMOTIVE ALLOCATION 1948
Stanier 3P 2-6-2T: 40190/1/2/4/8/9
Fairburn 4P 2-6-4T: 42158/59/78
Stanier 4P 2-6-4T: 42434/5/6/7/80/81/556
Stanier 8F 2-8-0: 48526/7/8/9/719/20
Fowler 7F 0-8-0: 49502/3/23/4/34/85/611/2/4/5/6/7/40/9
Barton Wright 2F 0-6-0ST: 51345/526
Aspinall 3F 0-6-0: 52160/71/244/96/317/34/6/68/99/460/7/522/41
Total: 53

LOSTOCK HALL M.P.D. LOCOMOTIVE ALLOCATION 1960
Stanier 3P 2-6-2T: 40183/92
Fairburn 4P 2-6-4T: 42158/87/286/96/8
Stanier 4P 2-6-4T: 42433/4/76/81/634/61/80/1
Aspinall 2F 0-6-0: 52290/429/45/56
 Riddles 'WD' 8F 2-8-0: 90258/66/77/95/331/5/67/413/541/56/658/75/81/9/720
Total: 34

LOSTOCK HALL M.P.D. LOCOMOTIVE ALLOCATION 1962
(Following closure of Preston shed)
Fairburn 4MT 2-6-4T: 42158/87/286/96/8
Stanier 4MT 2-6-4T: 42433/4/76/80/1/634/61
Ivatt 2MT 2-6-0: 46449,
Kitson 0P 0-4-0ST: 47002/8
Fowler 3F 0-6-0T: 47293/319/60/86/413/72/572
BR 2MT 2-6-0: 78036/7
 Riddles 'WD' 8F 2-8-0: 90258/66/77/95/335/541/84/658/75/81/9/713/20
Total: 38

LOSTOCK HALL M.P.D. LOCOMOTIVE ALLOCATION 31/12/1966
Fairburn 4MT 2-6-4T: 42187/224/97
Stanier 4MT 2-6-4T: 42546
Ivatt 4MT 2-6-0: 43019/41/6/118
Stanier 5MT 4-6-0: 44915/58/5107/97/226/347/402/21/44/50
Fowler 3F 0-6-0T: 47531
Stanier 8F 2-8-0: 48062/77/164/266/307/20/93/438/45/68/70/510/618/37/66/707/30/9
BR 2MT 2-6-0: 78020/1/37/41
Total: 41

LOSTOCK HALL M.P.D. LOCOMOTIVE ALLOCATION 04/08/1968
Stanier 5MT 4-6-0: 44713/806/888/910/971/5055/073/110/260/305/318/386/407/44
Stanier 8F 2-8-0: 48253/294/476/723/765
Total: 19

LOSTOCK HALL M.P.D. LOCOMOTIVE ALLOCATION 11/08/1968
Stanier 5MT 4-6-0: 45110/45305
Total: 2

One of the two class 0F Kitson four-coupled saddle tanks which came from Preston, 47008, stands on road 9 coupled to a Jinty and ready to be towed down to Greenbank yard for shunting duties on 15th June, 1963. This was one of the class to have extended bunkers and cut-back tank; her sister engine, 47002, retained her original design. *(Bob Watkinson)*

One of Speke Junction's numerous 9Fs, 92153 at Lostock Hall carriage sidings. *(Stan Withers)*

The old timber roof was long overdue for replacement after having been subject to damage from storms, decay and fires for over 70 years. Joe Brown, an ex-Lostock Hall fireman, recalled a particularly serious fire in 1952, when a sizeable area of the roof over roads 7 and 8 was destroyed:

'Someone left the blower full on and the timbers caught fire above a Lanky 3F loco. There were no hoses powerful enough to reach that height, so we formed a chain gang whereby buckets of water were passed up to a volunteer (me, who else would have been daft enough to do it?). I had to hurl the water uphill into the blazing timbers and dodge falling glass panes and burning spars, while getting soaked to the skin at the same time (No, I didn't get any extra pay for it!). One particularly large burning section of smoke ducting fell down and landed across the whistle chain of the engine beneath. The noise was deafening and we couldn't get near enough to stop it. The fire brigade was on its way, so we left it all to them'. - Can you imagine anything like this happening today?

On the subject of steam whistles, Joe Brown once had the honour of bringing in the New Year at Lostock Hall. It was a popular tradition in Preston that at the hour of midnight on December 31 each year, the men in charge of steam on the railways, docks and one or two factories would join together in welcoming the New Year with a loud and protracted chorus of steam whistles and sirens. At about 10 minutes to midnight, Joe went round some half dozen engines in the yard tying a large cob of coal to the whistle lever and resting the cob on a water gauge or steam valve. At midnight he then went round a second time, knocking each cob off its perch, thus creating a deafening noise which could be heard for miles around.

Ex-LYR class 2F saddle tank, 51423, was the last survivor of her class at Lostock Hall. She worked as shed pilot for most of the time, and occasionally shunted at Butler Street and Lostock Hall sorting sidings.*(E.H. Wood)*

The fire of '52 prompted remedial action and work commenced on a new steel-framed roof in August 1953. The length of the shed was cut back by 4 gabled sections, a distance of some 90 ft., leaving the walls in situ. The offices and workshops, however, remained as they were, beneath the original glazed and slated roofs. The height of the shed walls was increased and the south wall strengthened with concrete lintels to take the three 'H' section, steel framed roof trusses. It was a lightweight roof, with glazing bars either side of the galvanised steel smoke ducting and valley gutters. The whole was supported in the centre, between roads 4 and 5, by three steel girder stanchions. At the same time, improvements were carried out in the form of concrete surfacing, new wiring with power points on the support stanchions and electric lighting both inside and outside the shed. A brick bicycle shed

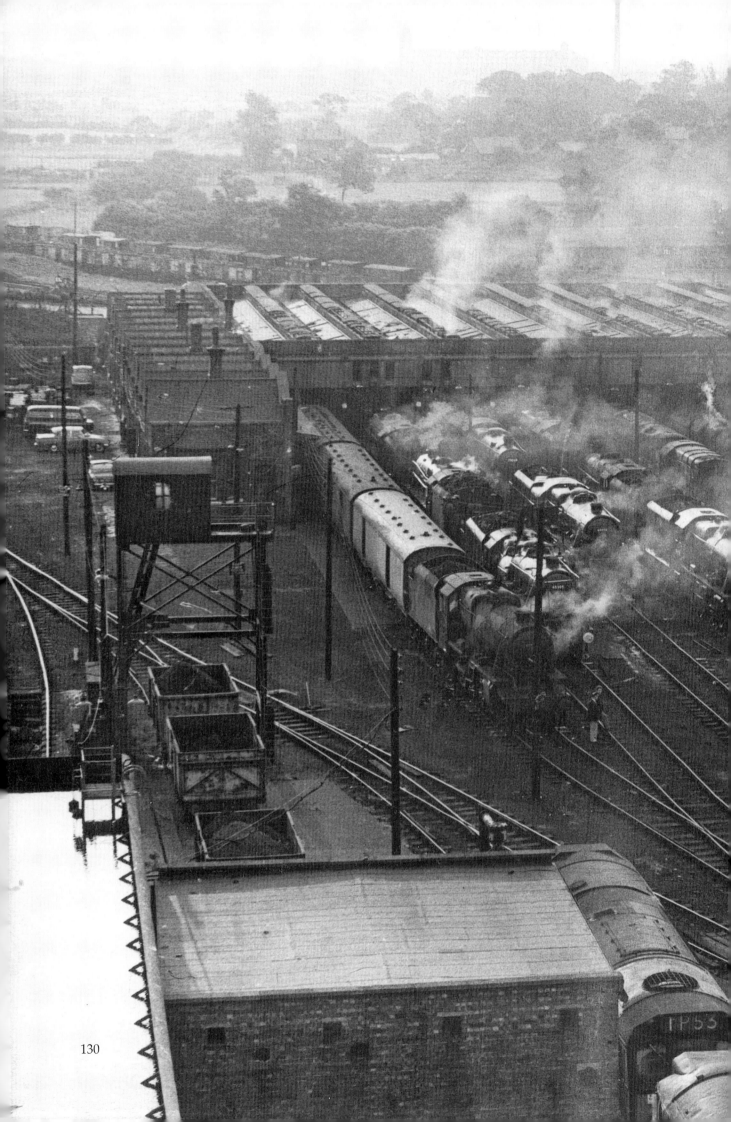

Engine shed and yard from the top of the coal hopper. *(Alan Castle)*

with six steel-framed windows and a lean-to corrugated asbestos roof was constructed at the rear of the main building. It was heated by a solid fuel stove, which was located in the centre, against the main wall. This building was also used for the storage of timber. A new drying and storage facility for sand was constructed and keyed-in to the western extremity of the south wall. This was quite a substantial two storey structure, being built of brick with large concrete lintels, steel-framed windows and a single pitch concrete roof.

It resembled one of those wartime coastal defense buildings, and was the last structure to be demolished on the site back in 1990. Such was its bulk, that it took the contractor the best part of two days to bring it level with the ground. This building measured 28 ft. x 26 ft. x 22 ft. 4 ins. at its highest point. Sand was shovelled from wagons on road 9 through two large openings on the first floor; it was then shovelled further onto an elevated section close to the heating apparatus, which dried the sand out, thus making it suitable for use on the locomotives. The rooms on the ground floor were used by the boiler washers and bar lads, and special lubricating and transmission oils were stored there in the 60's for the growing number of Diesel locomotives.

Many strange and remarkable initiation rituals were performed within these walls: cheeky young cleaners and firemen were known to have been buried up to their necks in sand and subjected to the 'coconut' treatment, by way of flying clogs and empty cans etc. The accompanying chants and intonations of Masters and Apprentices alike consisted of loud and protracted inflexions and variations, which echoed around the brick walls and poured forth through the open windows and far away beyond the printed word.

In 1953 a transverse partition was built in the oil and tool stores to serve as an office for the running foreman and a signing-on/off point. The top half of a large window on the external wall was bricked up and the remaining half modified for ease of verbal communication between the office and those outside. About this time, further experiments were being carried out with different types of fuel. Anthracite or hard coal was used for a time, as it is low in sulphur, high in carbon and burns well. Cannel coal or 'cannelite' is a highly volatile bituminous coal and burns at a very high temperature. Both types came in small rounded cobs and would have been more suitable for locomotives fitted with mechanical stokers, as footplate crews soon found themselves up to their knees in 'black cricket balls'. These experiments, like the oily coal combination, didn't last long, and the time-honoured regular steam coal continued to be used without any further messing.

Sir William Stanier was a remarkably handsome man and he designed some of the most remarkably handsome locomotives ever to grace the iron roads of this nation. The class 4MT 2-6-4 tank was one such magnificent example, and the perfect proportions are well illustrated in this picture. 42436, a long-serving Lostock Hall engine, stands on the disposal pit amid an assortment of shovels, fire-irons and barrows. The fitter's Bedford van can be seen in the background. *(David Burdon)*

On June 28, 1960, another big fire brought about more significant changes to Lostock Hall. This time it was a fire which destroyed the entire engine shed roof at Preston.[6] Ironically, just prior to this incident, British Railways had been making plans to transfer all the area motive power to Preston and close the shed at Lostock Hall. The staff at Preston struggled on under appalling conditions until the shed was closed down altogether on September 12, 1961. The locomotives and staff were distributed to other sheds in the area, including Wigan, Blackpool and Lostock Hall. Fate had brought about a complete reversal of plans: not only had Lostock Hall been given a new lease of life, but also the allocation of locomotives and staff had been substantially increased.

From an enthusiast's point of view, a visit to the shed was from now on an opportunity to get a close up of a number of Jubilee, Patriot, Scot, Coronation and Britannia pacific classes - something hitherto deemed unthinkable at a place which had always been regarded as just another 'Lanky goods shed'. Other newcomers to the shed included ex-LNW class G2a, 0-8-0 'Super D's' and ex-LMS class 0F, 0-4-0 Kitson saddle tanks. The former were used mainly on Wigan coal traffic and the Ribble Dock branch. Although powerful and reliable, they were not favoured by the Lostock Hall men and soon found their way to other sheds or consigned to road 9. The latter were specifically used for shunting around the short radius curves at Greenbank goods yard. These small tanks had to be towed to work and back by a larger engine - on most occasions a Jinty - owing to the short wheelbase failing to register on the track circuit system.

Jubilee class 6P5F, 45590 Travancore, looking good after some
attention from the cleaners on May 8, 1962. *(Tony Gillett)*

For a brief period, Lostock Hall men found themselves being rostered on distance routes to Glasgow and Euston. Duties on excursion and relief trains worked by Scots and Jubilees were also routine. Of course it wasn't all roses for the indigenous staff at 24C: there were frequent grumblings about their having to take orders from these 'foreign' senior men, foremen and supervisors from Preston (the old LYR/LNWR rivalry continued right up to the bitter end). The year 1961 saw the retirement of long-serving shed master, Jimmy Turner. His successor was Harold Sedgebeer, an ex-Somerset & Dorset man, who had previously worked at Skipton. He was getting on in years, but it didn't stop him riding to work and back on a BSA Bantam motor bike. His pride and joy at the shed was the breakdown crane and attendant tool vans, and he was always keen to travel with his number one crane operator, Harold Martin, to the scene of any mishaps and supervise the lifting operations. The crane was a steam-powered Cowens Sheldon design of 50 tons, number RS100150, which had come from Carlisle Kingmoor shed. As with all the other cranes it was painted black, but in 1961 it was sent to Derby to be re-painted, as red was to become the standard colour for all steam cranes; but Harold insisted that his crane was to be painted in Midland Railway maroon and lined out.

A broadside view of the Lostock Hall breakdown crane, at the scene of the Hest Bank derailment which occurred on 20th May, 1965. *(Bill Ashcroft)*

He went further to insist that the legend on the side was to read: 'Lostock Hall Motive Power Section', instead of 'depot'. All this was carried out in the Derby paint shop at King Harry's behest, and Lostock Hall ended up with a unique and smart-looking crane. It took pride of place on road one, close to Harry's office, so he could keep a wary eye on it. One day a young cleaner was shunting the crane into the shed; careful as he was, however, he misjudged the distance and pushed it a little too far. The back wheels jumped the ramps and landed on the floor with a crash. Unfortunately, Harry had emerged from his office to observe the operation, and on seeing the calamity, he grabbed the young lad by his dungaree braces and bundled him along to the back of the shed, where he pointed to the scene of sacrilege and shouted, *'Look what you've done, you irresponsible little ....!'*

The Preston crane arrived at Lostock Hall in 1961, but didn't stay long and was taken away to Gloucester. The Lostock Hall crane was transferred to Wigan Springs Branch in 1968 and is now preserved at the Midland Railway Centre in Butterley. [7]

Following instructions from the divisional manager, Harold Sedgebeer had some makeshift signs made to warn enginemen about creating too much smoke. The signs read 'WATCH THAT SMOKE' and 'KEEP THAT SMOKE DOWN', and were strategically nailed to poles around the yard. One day, driver Tommy Robinson and his mate were preparing an engine just outside the shed and making a lot of clag in the process. On seeing this, Mr Sedgebeer came across and shouted, *'You're making too much smoke, Mr. Robinson! Can't you read the sign?'* Driver Robinson stuck his head out of the cab and looking round, he replied, *'I can't see anything for all this smoke.'* *'The sign says watch that smoke!'* retorted Mr. Sedgebeer. *'I am doing, Mr. Sedgebeer, I'm stood 'ere watchin' it,'* came the droll reply. The old gaffer gave up and went back to his office.

In September 1963, the shed code was changed for the last time, becoming 10D, a sub shed of Carnforth. By this time all the LYR locomotives had gone, leaving one or two Midland types as the last of the old-timers. Among these were a couple of 3F, 0-6-0 Jinty tanks, 47201 and 47211, the latter retaining the condensing pipes from her early years as a London engine. The two Kitson 0F 's, 47002 and 47008 remained in service until 1964, and the Austerity 2-8-0's were fast giving place to the more popular and reliable Stanier types, having all disappeared by the end of 1965. Around this time, the shed was allocated a Bedford 10.5 CWT. Type CA van. This was used by the fitters for the collection of components from Horwich and for emergency trips to breakdown locations etc. A number of Diesel locomotives arrived from Preston in 1961, comprising half a dozen class 08 six-coupled shunters and a brace of Yorkshire Engine Co. 0-4-0 shunters, D2862 and 2868. The former was used for shunting at the C&W shops and the latter replaced the Kitson tank on the Greenbank shunt.

Modern traction driver and maintenance training commenced at the shed, following the arrival of one or two larger type 2 locomotives in the mid 60's, and later on, one of the new D400 class locos, D403, was allocated to the shed for training purposes. Safety and awareness instruction courses commenced at the shed for enginemen travelling beneath the high-voltage wires between Crewe and London. Three gallows-like structures were erected over the track between the shed and station platform and rigged up with dead cable.

The three tank wagons which constituted the improvised Diesel fuelling point. They are reputed to have come from the gas works at Lostock Hall, where they were used for the conveyance of hot tar. *(Author's collection)*

Young firemen in particular had to learn the dangers involved in climbing above footplate level when handling lamps, shovels and fire-irons. A makeshift Diesel fuelling point was put together between roads 8 and 9, in front of the grounded coach body. It consisted of 3 redundant 4-wheeled gas-tankers, which are reputed to have come from Lostock Hall gas works.

They were located on two standard lengths of bullhead rail, which were loosely laid on their sides upon a row of sleepers and kept in place with 12 inch iron nails and wooden chocks. The early 60's saw the arrival of standard class 2MT lightweight 2-6-0's at the shed. These engines were used on local passenger services, shunting and carriage heating duties at Preston Station. On Sunday September 6, 1964, two of these locos, 78040 and 78041, sharing a specially made 'Last Day' headboard, worked trains both ways between Preston and Southport. The very last passenger train of the day, the 10.20 pm from Southport to Preston was hauled by 10D Fairburn tank, 42296, with driver Harry Moulding doing the honours. 42296 was reckoned to have been the best engine of her class at the shed, and driver Ernie Heyes once said that she would steam at the sight of a shovel. Lostock Hall engines had a reputation for working 'last one's', and it all began on Saturday, May 31, 1930, when ex-LYR 2-4-2 radial tank, No. 10646 hauled the last passenger service train from Longridge to Preston. The train left Longridge at 9.58 pm amid blasts on the steam whistle and exploding fog signals. At Grimsargh, driver Billington of Lostock Hall shook hands with the station master, Harold Latham, and wished him well on his retirement.

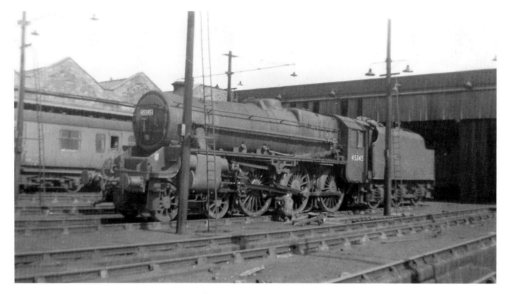

Class 5MT 45345 receives a new brake block for the middle driver on a quiet Sunday afternoon in March 1968.
(Author)

With time running out for steam, Stanier Big Eight, 48723, back-shunts a rake of wagons into the C&W works sidings on 31st July, 1968. Joe Booth is at the controls. *(Author)*

The closure of a number of steam sheds in the South and Midlands and the disposal of redundant motive power there and in other parts of the country, resulted in an assortment of locomotives arriving at the remaining depots in the north-west. Among these arrivals at Lostock Hall was an initial batch of four Ivatt class 4MT 2-6-0's.

These engines, like so many other 'foreigners' in the past, were not looked upon too favourably by the enginemen and were given nicknames such as 'Flying Pigs' and 'Coffee-pots,' these being some of the kinder appellations. They were heavily run down and were to be seen in appalling condition on their removal to the scrap sidings. One of the class, 43106, which retained her Midland & Great Northern staff catching apparatus, survived the death sentence and left 10D for the last time on July 30, 1968 bound for Bridgenorth and a brighter future on the Severn Valley Railway.

The Britannia Pacifics found themselves being relocated to sheds in the North West, namely Crewe North and Carlisle Kingmoor. Although none were ever officially allocated to Lostock Hall, a number of them spent some weeks at a time there when working the West Coast main line. The regular ones included 70017/19/25/26/29 and 44. 70017, Arrow was wrecked in an accident at Bog Junction on the through goods line at Carlisle in 1966. A signal was passed at danger and the engine ran into the back of a ballast train. Fortunately nobody was hurt, but Arrow was a write off and spent some time in store at Upperby, prior to being towed away for scrap. Other BR standard types which arrived at the shed in the mid-60's included one or two 9F's, which didn't last there long, and a batch of four class two 2-6-2 tanks, numbers 84010, 84016 from Fleetwood and 84015, 84028 from Skipton. These push and pull tanks were never used and were stored by the goods shed for a while before being taken away for scrap, more the tragedy as they were all in good condition with relatively low mileage.

At around the same time, a batch of three BR standard 4MT 2-6-4 tanks, 80056, 80125 and 80129, arrived at the shed from Carlisle. They were in ex-works condition, but unfortunately they had been towed all that way without the connecting rods having been removed first.

On examining the motion, the rods were found to be buckled and subsequently, as there were no spares available, the engines were condemned. The last major structural alteration at Lostock Hall, prior to its closure as a steam shed, took place in February 1967, when a rake of locomotives was being shunted into the shed on road 2. The driver, ex-Stockport man Mick Bowden, misinterpreted the signal given him by the lookout man and pushed the engines too far, causing the tender of the rear engine, Black 5, 45339, to jump the ramps and bulldoze its way through the back wall. Fortunately, during the reconstruction of the roof in 1953, provision had been made for such an eventuality, by building up the wall with non-keyed panels or vertical joints at the end of each road and laying a pre-stressed concrete lintel between each panel and the shed roof. The falling masonry caused damage to a new radiator for the shed's 0-4-0 Diesel shunter and a Reliant glass-fibre 3-wheeler, which belonged to fitter's mate, Billy Moat. This was the second such vehicle to suffer damage under similar circumstances - Lostock Hall was not a safe place to park a 'rubber duck'.

Shortly after this event, some mischievous member of staff daubed the epitaph 'Bowden's Gap' by the new entrance. It was later followed by the prophecy, 'The shape of sheds to come'. Unfortunately, there were to be no more sheds as such, but Mick Bowden's creative work is still talked about to this day. The brickwork was tidied up and the 'gap' remained as it was until the 1970's, when two timber-framed doors cladded with aluminium sheets were fitted for security and staff comfort during the Winter months. According to Bill Wilson there had been previous instances of engines (and a breakdown crane) running through the back wall. One outstanding example occurred back in the early 1920's, when a young fireman called 'Ginger' Gregson brought an Aspinall 0-6-0 back to the shed single handed. To save time and effort, he tried to do something which he had seen done by others on several occasions: he cracked the regulator open just enough to keep the engine crawling forward, while he climbed down to set the points then, after allowing the engine to pass over, he switched them back and ran up to the second set of points. This time, it didn't work out right; the engine suddenly began to gather speed, and try as he might, he couldn't catch up with it. The engine collided with a dead member of its class at the back of the shed and shoved it through the wall adjacent to the toilet block. One of the fitters who had been working on that engine and another member of staff who had been on the throne at the time, had much to say about the matter, the content of which cannot be recorded here. A lesson had been learned and the art of moving driverless engines over points was left to the more senior members of staff, and the likes of Buster Keaton.

The famous Bowden's Gap at the end of road two. *(Tom Heavyside)*

As the sheds began to close in the North West, more locomotives and men arrived at Lostock Hall. Owing to the dwindling supply of parts at Crewe and Horwich works, steam locomotives with non-critical defects were condemned and replaced by engines from other depots and, in the meantime, those on the scrap sidings were cannibalised by the fitters to keep the others going.

The surviving engines were in a sorry state and it became obvious that the days of steam traction on BR were numbered. Following the closure of Kirkby Stephen shed, driver Bob Barker was transferred to Lostock Hall, and when he arrived at the shed, driver Bill Wilson took it upon himself to give him a guided tour and introduced him to other members of staff. In later years, Bob spoke highly of Bill Wilson's kindness and regarded Lostock Hall as being a 'friendly place to work'.

Other men continued to arrive from Blackpool, Southport and Lower Darwen sheds and they could clearly see that the big decline was not confined to steam traction; they only had to look around at the decrepit state of the infrastructure and read the closure proposals etc. to realise that they were facing an uncertain future. By the end of 1967, all the Stanier and Fairburn tanks had been withdrawn, together with the 2MT, 2-6-0 's, leaving an allocation of Black 5's, 8F's and 4MT, 2-6-0's. The radius of activity had been narrowed down to Lancashire and West Yorkshire, with only a few passenger turns.

The last surviving Ivatt class 4MT, 43106, being prepared for her journey to Bridgenorth and preservation on the Severn Valley Railway, 31st July 1968. *(Author)*

A row of four class 2, 2-6-2 tanks, in store alongside the goods shed, before the final trip to the breaker's yard. The station signal box is in the background. (Alan Castle)

1968 was the last year of BR steam, and by the end of June that year, only three sheds remained open for the servicing of steam locomotives: Carnforth, Lostock Hall and Rose Grove. People began arriving in Lancashire from all over the country to capture the euphoria of those final days. Lostock Hall had never before seen so many visitors: those who lived far afield and without the means to afford bed and breakfast and long repetitive journeys, slept rough in brake vans and waiting rooms.

Tents sprouted up on waste-land and battered old vans were to be seen parked up on the side roads, their bearded occupants messing about with cameras and recorders and cooking tinned food on a primus stove. Much has been written of those final months in which the men and locomotives of Lostock Hall played so great a part. The following provides a detailed account of events which found their place in the annals of British railway history.

A Black 5 line-up at the shed with left to right: 44888, 45260 and 44806. *(J. Suter)*

The beginning of the end came on Friday, August 2, when Black 5, 44878 became the last steam locomotive to work a section of the Longridge branch, with a trip to Courtaulds sidings at Red Scar and back. The driver was Lostock Hall man, Ernie Heyes, who went on to make history the following day. On the evening of Saturday, August 3, 1968, an unusually clean Black 5, 45212 left Lostock Hall shed for Preston station.

Crowds were already gathering as the engine cleared the main island platform and reversed into the 'Derby bay', to await the 5.05 pm. from Euston. The front portion of this train was for Glasgow and the rear portion for the 8.50 pm. to Blackpool South. With the Diesel-hauled front portion out of the way, driver Bob Barker reversed 45212 up to the coaches and his fireman, Mel Rigby, climbed down and coupled-up. After signing autographs and posing for the photographers, Bob and his mate got the train underway amid tumultuous cheers, exploding fog signals and an electric storm of flash-bulbs. This was the penultimate steam-hauled passenger train on BR standard gauge metals. While this was going on, another Black 5, 45318 had arrived at Preston from Lostock Hall tender first and was waiting in the bay platform at the south end of the station for the 5.25 pm. from Glasgow. When the train arrived, the front portion was uncoupled and taken on its way to Manchester. The rear portion was for the 9.25 pm. to Liverpool Exchange, and this service would normally have been allocated to a type 4 English Electric Diesel, but, as in the case of the previous train, and for some unknown reason, such a locomotive was not available that evening.

Driver Ernie Heyes and fireman Tony Smith likewise received the celebrity treatment as they prepared the engine for that final memorable journey along the South Lancashire plain. For the second time that evening a train set off to the accompaniment of loud hurrahs, explosions and dazzling flashbulbs.

The carriages were absolutely packed, with standing room only and people were leaning out of the windows exchanging farewells with those on the platforms. As the red tail light disappeared into the twilight, it took some coming to terms with the fact that this was the very last officially scheduled, steam-hauled passenger service train to run on BR standard gauge tracks. It was the sad end of an era which had begun some 140 years ago, just a few miles down the road at Rainhill.

Back at Lostock Hall shed, a number of dedicated volunteers were hard at work with buckets of Diesel oil and rags, cleaning up a batch of some 13 steam locomotives in preparation for the following day's events: the six chartered 'end of steam' specials. The engines took on that 'ex-works' appearance as they gleamed in the lamp light - a sharp contrast to the dark mass of condemned engines on the scrap sidings. Buffer beams and number plates were carefully repainted and the lining on cab-sides and tenders was made visible again by rubbing away the shop paint and grime with the serrated edge of a half-crown piece.

While this was going on, 45212 returned to Preston and commenced shunting and steam-heating sleeper carriages. She must have returned to the shed and then gone back to Preston later on the following day, as she was seen and photographed working the 'station shunt' around 3.00 pm. on August 4th. This made her famous as she had now become the last standard gauge steam loco to work a normal roster for BR. Mercifully she was saved from the breaker's yard along with other Lostock Hall Black 5's, 45000, 45305, 45407, 44806 and 45110.

Lostock Hall driver, Billy Bamber, is standing easy in the doorway of 45017, as the Stockport pilot takes over the controls during the course of an August 4th special. His fireman, Joe Unsworth, is just visible behind the pilot. *(Courtesy, John Bargh)*

On the morning of August 4, the engines, all looking their Sunday best, left the shed in two's and three's to work the six special trains, which all ran within the borders of the Manchester and Preston Divisional Areas. The engines involved that day were: 45156, Ayrshire Yeomanry (minus nameplates) on 1T80; 45305 on 1T85; 48476 working double-headed with Carnforth standard 5, 73069 on 1L50; 45407 working double-headed with Carnforth standard 73069 on the second stage of 1L50; 70013, Oliver Cromwell on stage 3 of 1L50, later to work 1Z74 in tandem with 44781, which was, in turn, later to work double-headed with Rose Grove 8F 48773 on stage 2 of the same special and stage 3 being worked double-headed by Carnforth engines 45390 and 45025; 44871 and 44894 working together on 1Z78; 44874 working double-headed with 45017 on 1Z79.

That same morning, 8F, 48493 left the shed to work a ballast shunt at Farington Junction yard. This was to be the last freight handling as such to be carried out by a Lostock Hall steam locomotive.

The engines began to return to the shed later on in the afternoon. 70013 was late back due to a four hour delay in Manchester, but the last one to return was 45156 with driver Andy Hall, arriving back at the shed at around 4.00 a.m. on the following morning. That was the official end of steam traction at Lostock Hall after some 87 years and the shed was closed as a motive power depot on that day, Monday, August 5 1968. Going back to the previous evening, class 8F engine, No 48773, with driver Arnold Hodgson and fireman Jim Walker, arrived at Preston Station around 7.00 p.m. returning light-engine from Carnforth to Rose Grove. After stopping briefly at platform 9 to drop off the crew of Black 5, 44781, they continued their journey via Todd Lane Junction and Bamber Bridge, and this must have been the last steam locomotive to run the full length of the former 'Preston Extension'. Her arrival heralded the end of an era in East Lancashire, as she was the last engine to have her fire dropped at Rose Grove shed, with Jim Walker doing the honours. Thankfully, the 'big eight' is now preserved, and Jim still reflects on his footplate career and that final day with mixed feelings of pride and melancholy.

Monday, August 5, 1968, and class 8F, 48546, stands cold, silent and redundant on road 10; the contents of her tender, for which she will have no further use, piled up alongside. The coal was later bagged up and given out to the elderly folks of the town as a gesture of good will. *(Author)*

The shed master, Harold Sedgebeer retired on August 5th, and Freddy Swindles took over under the new title of Depot Manager. Those members of the footplate staff who had not been made redundant were transferred to a signing-on point at Preston, leaving a few members of the maintenance staff at the shed to work on modern traction. It was, however, not entirely the end, for three days later, on Wednesday August 7th, Britannia Pacific, No 70013, Oliver Cromwell and Black 5, No 44871 were prepared at Lostock Hall and left the shed in tandem for Carnforth via Lostock Hall Junction, Todd Lane and Butler Street, as part of the preparations for the BR 'Farewell to Steam' 15 Guinea Special, which was scheduled to run on Sunday, August 11th.

On the evening of Saturday, August 10th, clouds of smoke and steam were visible again at Lostock Hall shed, when 70013 arrived light engine from Carnforth, in readiness for an early start on the outward journey of the following day's Special from Manchester Victoria to Carlisle. Two Black 5's, 45305 and 45110 were prepared at Lostock Hall for the occasion. 45305 was to have taken the special, 1T57, on the first leg of the journey from Liverpool Lime Street to Manchester Victoria, but this duty fell to her stable mate 45110, after it was discovered that the former's brick arch had collapsed in the firebox. These were the last engines to have their fires raised at the shed. Driver, Bill Wilson and fireman, Jim Marlor (both of whom had to stand in at short notice for the booked crew) took the loco to Liverpool tender-first.

At the end of the day, 70013, which had travelled light from Carlisle via the Long Drag, called in briefly at Lostock Hall for coal, water and turning before continuing her journey south. She was, in all probability, the last steam loco to use the shed's turntable. 45110 with driver Ken Mason and fireman Roger (Dickie) Owen, travelled on the last leg of 1T57 from Manchester to Liverpool Lime Street, then took over and worked light-engine back to Lostock Hall via Edge Hill.

As 45110 left the platform, with a couple of Edge Hill crews on the footplate cadging a lift back to their shed, one of these men, fireman Stephen Roberts, on noticing a man on the platform with a microphone in his hand, raised his arms and shouted the immortal words, "No more dirty hands!".

When the engine arrived back on shed at 12.49 pm., fireman Tom Jones and his mate Jimmy Slater took care of the disposal operation, during the course of which, Tom had to move the engine from the ash pits to road five, and by so doing, in the early hours of Monday, August 12th, he became the last man to drive a steam locomotive at Lostock Hall engine shed.

Tom (Eric) Jones had been working as a cleaner at the shed around the time that another man with the same name was making an impression in the popular music industry. This became an integral part of an anecdote which runs thus: Tom was working the night shift when, sometime around midnight, he ran out of fags. There were no shops or pubs open at that time in those days, so he had to nip down to the village where there was a cigarette vending machine outside the Pleasant Retreat pub. Tom had rolled his coppers through the slot and was in the process of pulling out the magic drawer, when a copper of a different kind rolled up in a van and asked him what he was doing there, messing about with the machine at that ungodly hour.

Tom explained as best he could, then the Policeman asked him his name. The fun started when Tom gave him an honest answer, to which the officer rejoined, *'Oh yes? And my name's Elvis Presley. You'd better come along with me'*. He then ran Tom in to Leyland Police Station.

Barney Campbell was foreman that night and he'd been looking round the shed for Tom. He had just returned to his office when the phone rang. An authoritative voice at the other end enquired as to whether he had a Tom Jones on his books. When Barny answered in the affirmative, there was an awkward silence, then the crest-fallen sergeant explained the situation and added, *'Can you send someone over to pick him up?'*

Now Barny was normally a very placid and easy-going man and accordingly earned the respect of all those who had the privilege of working with him, but on this occasion he went ballistic: *'Now look here,'* he shouted, *'you took him away and you can bloody well bring him back; and be sharp about it, as I've got a job for him to do!'* They were happy days while they lasted.

Lostock Hall driver, Cliff Nelson (left) and his fireman,
John Fletcher on the footplate of 45073 on 19th July 1968. *(Bill Ashcroft)*

Closure and dereliction, April 2nd, 1988. An abandoned two-wheeled dog cart from the fitter's shop, and an axle from a 20 ton brake van in the background, a reminder of the shed's final role as a C&W works. *(Author)*

Lines of Stanier Black 5 and 8F locomotives at Lostock Hall await the cutters torch, 4th August 1968 *(Peter Brumby)*

Post Steam Period

As early as March, 1961, BR had drawn up plans for a new shed and stabling point for Diesel multiple-units. This would have been quite an impressive layout if it had materialised: An eight road shed was designed with the tracks set further apart than those in the steam shed. The new building would have been located immediately south of and at an angle of 12 degrees to the existing shed, with workshops and staff facilities to the rear. At the same time, alterations were to be made to the LYR building, whereby the sand stores and bicycle shed would have been demolished and a new bicycle shed built against the south wall. Road 8 was to be modified for use as a fuelling point for Diesel shunters. A stabling point with six sidings and low concrete platforms for 6 and 4-car multiple units would have been located to the south-west of the new shed, complete with three sidings for fuel and water storage. Further to this, a site had been marked out for a future wagon maintenance works adjacent to the carriage sheds, and a freight-liner depot serving the Leyland Motors factory nearby.

A revised plan was drawn up for Lostock Hall in 1969, for the construction of the proposed Preston-Farington Joint Maintenance Depot. This would have involved the complete demolition of the steam shed and the construction of a six road shed for fuel and inspection, wagon maintenance and repairs. A large area was also marked out for the District Civil Engineer's stores. The plans were optimistic to say the least at a time when the freight service was in rapid decline, and much humbler and tentative proposals had to be considered. Following the end of steam traction, the shed building, which was already beginning to look decrepit and run-down, was utilised as a fuel and inspection

John Fletcher again: this time on the driver's side of preserved Black 5, 45231, at Blackburn on September 23, 2009, still working on the footplate some 41 years on after the official end of steam traction on BR. With him is fellow 10D fireman, Paul Tuson. *(Paul Tuson collection)*

depot, as there were no such facilities at Preston. It was also used as a temporary storage depot for permanent way machinery and ballast trucks. Work carried on there until September, 1972, when all area servicing was transferred to Wigan. Locomotive fitter, Fred Parker, was the last of the 'steam men' to leave the depot after working the 14.00 to 22.00 shift on fuel and inspection duty, thus bringing to a close the building's association with motive power after 90 years.

The shed was then used for the maintenance, repair and scrapping of carriages and wagons which carried on for some years until a fire destroyed a section of roof covering roads 3 to 8. The two surviving roads were partitioned off and business resumed, carrying on until 1988, when the shed was closed down altogether and became derelict. The long process of demolition work on the vandalised building began in June 1989 and was completed by February 1990. BR had considered keeping part of the building for the storage of track maintenance vehicles, but the surveyor's report indicated critical structural damage to the south wall. This had most likely occurred as a result of a design fault on the replacement roof, whereby inadequate load-bearing support had been provided in the central area, and the fact that the above mentioned fire had caused the transverse beams to expand, thus exerting lateral pressure on the wall. Whichever way you look at it, the 1950's steel roof, as with similar concrete structures at Carnforth and Rose Grove, was only designed to last a maximum of 30 years.

1968 was not just the end of the line for the steam locomotive, it was the end of a way of life for the railway community at Lostock Hall, as it was with many other communities which had developed around the industries they served. It was a time to move on and seek alternative employment, with many of the former shed staff finding work at Leyland Motors and Royal Mail. Within the following five years, many more were to lose their jobs owing to a decline in freight traffic, the de-staffing of intermediate stations; the closure of the line from Bamber Bridge to Preston via Todd Lane Junction and the transfer of all signalling and point operations to a central power box in Preston. By 1973, the railway system around Preston had become a mere shadow of its former self and for those who survived the redundancies, life on the railway would never be the same again.

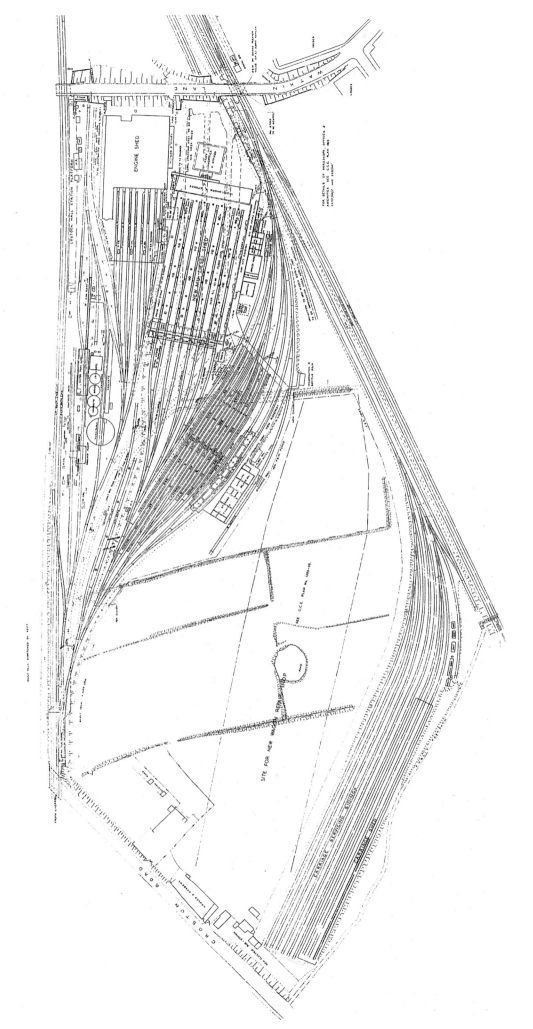

Plan No. 55503 is the original proposed Diesel and multiple unit depot, which I think is dated 1961. *(National Railway Museum, York)*

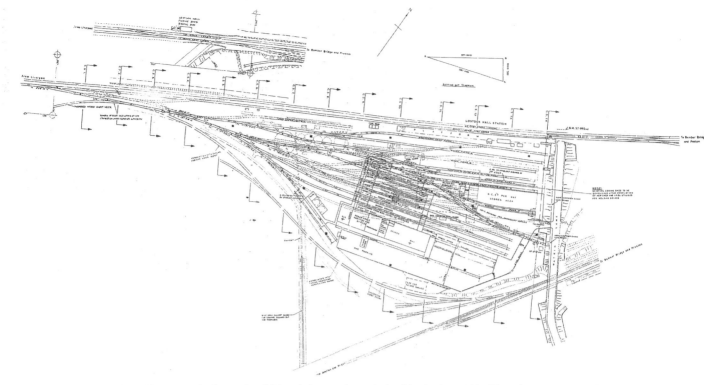

Plan No 80934 is the revised Diesel depot plan, drafted in the late 60's. The plans were much attenuated in the wake of closures and a decline in the freight service.
(National Railway Museum, York)

Lostock Hall shed foreman, Barny Campbell with the lock and key from the shedmaster's door, which were salvaged by the author during the demolition of the building in 1990. On the right is Lostock Hall and Preston driver, Vinny Commons, with Lostock Hall and Crewe driver, Bert Stewart in the middle. The picture was taken at the Witton Country Park Exhibition Centre, near Blackburn. The two organisers at the back are John Bentley, right, and the author. The exhibition was held to commemorate the 25th anniversary of the shed's closure to steam traction. *(Lancashire Evening Telegraph)*

FOOTNOTES

[1] Preston Guardian, June 10th 1882.

[2] ibid.

[3] ibid.

[4] Driver Redford was involved in an accident at Blackburn station, on August 8th, 1881, when the Manchester to Hellifield express collided with his engine, Vesuvius, at around 3.15 pm. The engine was pushed back into the carriage he was shunting, and such were the injuries he received (compound fracture to the right leg), that he was unable to work on the footplate again. He will be best remembered for the photographs he took of the ELR locomotives.
  Driver Bullfield had also been involved in a serious accident, this one being the collision at Burscough Junction on January 15th 1880, in which 5 people were killed, including his fireman, Robert Clarkson.

[5] L.M&S.R. Reorganisation of the Motive Power Depot. The Railway gazette, 1937. The organisation introduced on the LMS was known as the "Motive Power Area Locomotive Supply, Repair, Concentration and Garage Scheme."

[6] The fire was accidentally started by passed cleaner, Jack Cray, who had been preparing a Super D in the shed for a trip on the 'Pilling Pig' (Preston to Pilling coal train). There was a lot of coal dust in the tender, and this came out of the chimney in a shower of sparks, which subsequently ignited the roof-timbers.

[7] The Preston break-down crane was a 1913 LNWR design, No RS1009, of 36 tons. It was transferred to Gloucester Barnwood Depot on the Western Region in 1962. The ex-Kingmoor crane at Lostock Hall, No RS1001, cost £5,547 to build. It had gone to Kingmoor from Durran Hill in 1936; and before that it was allocated to New Carlisle. At Lostock hall it came under the Preston Division, and its radius of activity included: Kirkham North Jct. and Blackpool South via Marton and Lytham; Poulton & Blackpool North; Moss Lane Jct. and Cliviger East inclusive; Rose Grove West & Padiham; Farington Curve Jct.; Lostock Hall / Engine Shed; Todd Lane Jct. & Lostock Hall Jct.; Preston E.L & Butler Street Goods & Bamber bridge Jct.; Lower Darwen inclusive & Blackburn; Cherry Tree Jct. & Feniscowles; Gannow Jct. & Skipton exclusive; Daisyfield Jct. & Hellifield exclusive; Accrington West Jct. & North Jct. & South Jct. inclusive; Euxton Jct. & Horwich Fork Jct. inclusive; Horwich Branch; Burscough South Jct. (Information kindly provided by Mel Parker)

CHAPTER TEN

Travelling East

Preston Junction, Bamber Bridge & Hoghton

The station at Todd Lane had an island platform with a short bay adjacent to the Preston line, which originally served as a locomotive neck for the assistance of heavy trains up the bank to Blackburn. There was also a carriage siding on the junction curve and a loop to the south of the station (see chapter one). Facilities for newspapers and parcels existed, but not for goods. The name was changed to Todd Lane junction in 1952.

Access to the platform was by way of a steep staircase from the three-arched Todd Lane road bridge. It was built of brick with sandstone steps and half-way landing, with accommodation beneath for a lamp room and cold water stand-pipe. The station buildings comprised four separate blocks built of red Accrington brick, the gangways between being wide enough for the storage of platform trucks etc. The first block (facing the bridge) contained the booking office with a room for the station master and parcels facilities; the second served as a general waiting room and porter's office; the third contained the ladies waiting room with wash room facilities, and the fourth was the gentlemen's lavatory (see drawings).

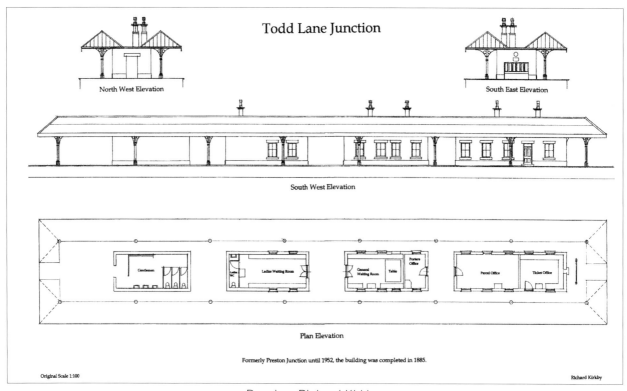

Drawing: Richard Kirkby

This staff photo from 1903 used to hang on the booking office wall at Preston Junction, and by some miracle it has survived. There are eight names on the reverse and I can only assume they are given left to right, starting with the back row: J. Hale, J. Grisdale, Waddington (Stationmaster), S. Hulton, Ainsworth, Harrison, Morgan, W. Dickenson. *(Courtesy Chris Canner)*

The booking office was the only building on the station to have a cellar, and during the course of the demolition process, many old ledgers and rolls of advertising posters and time tables were removed from there and burned on site. A glazed, wrought-iron canopy with eight cast-iron stanchions on each side, covered the entire length of the buildings. The glazing was removed during he last war and never replaced, the frames being covered with boards and bitumen felted. A 1903 group photo on the booking office wall showed a staff of nine; this number had dwindled down to four by 1965, with three porters and the station master, Bill Wright, who was also in charge of the station at Bamber Bridge.

By the end of 1966 there was just one man left to look after the station, a long-serving and well respected character called Arthur Bennett. He will be best remembered for his stentorian announcements on the arrival of east-bound passenger trains: *'All stations to Blackburn, Burnley and beyond!!'*, or, on some occasions, *'Up yonder!!'*, instead of *'beyond'*. He left the uninitiated wondering if only unchartered territory lay beyond Burnley. Arthur went on to take charge of Bamber Bridge station following the closure of Todd Lane on September 4, 1972. His signature announcement there was *'Bamber!!....Bamber!!'*

Jubilee, 45694 Bellerophon, passes the gas works junction signals on the approach to Todd Lane Junction with a Bradford to Blackpool seasonal extra. *(Arthur Haymes)*

Ticket & Price *(Author)*

The signal box at Todd Lane controlled the junction for Brownedge Crossing and Lostock Hall Junction. It also controlled the exit from a Goods Loop, adjacent to the former ticket platform. It was a Railway Signal Company (RSCo.) timber cabin with a 36 lever frame of the same manufacturer. This signal box controlled the electric lock of the ground frame at the Gas Works and also the bolt lock of the 'Preston Junction G.F.' (called Preston Junction Carriage Shed Sidings, in the sectional appendix). It remained in use until 1972 and the introduction of the Preston PSB.

The Preston Junction G.F. (later called Todd Lane Junction Carriage Sidings G.F.) controlled the points which served a carriage siding on the left side of the Preston Junction curve. This was originally a four-lever frame, being reduced to two levers sometime after 1934. It was decommissioned on February 9th, 1969.

There were special instructions for Preston Junction that stated, *'Passenger trains for E.L. direction requiring assistance must stop at Preston Junction to attach the assistant engine'.* [1]

The ubiquitous Lanky saddle tank, 51423, hurries towards Preston Junction station on her way back to Lostock Hall shed, after a shunting turn at Butler Street in 1951. The elevated concrete ducting for the signal telegraph cable is in place on the embankment, and the old timber poles will soon disappear. *(Author's collection)*

The Preston end of Todd Lane station as seen from the footplate of Austerity, 90675. *(Alan Castle)*

Up Passenger Workings at Preston Junction

The following table shows typical passenger workings at Preston Junction; from here workings would split at the junction to work east, mainly Accrington or west, mainly Liverpool.

Of special interest are a number of empty stock workings to and from Preston Junction; one working in particular arrives late at night 11.4 pm (SX) and 11.19 pm. (SO) to be stabled in the carriage siding at Preston Junction, with the engine working light to Lostock Hall shed at 11.15 pm. (SX), although there is no mention in the timetable how the engine is disposed of on Saturdays. The Working Time Table for July 6th to September 27th 1936 (prior period to the one displayed) has the light engine movement as daily, but on Saturdays this would work out before the train had arrived!

This empty stock appears to form the 5.35 am. from Preston Junction to Croston and there are no light engine movements for this working. It should be noticed that the carriage siding at Preston Junction can only be accessed from the Up line (Preston Junction to Lostock Hall Junction), therefore the engine would be at the Lostock Hall end of the train, so any onward working must continue in that direction, hence the somewhat bizarre working.

September 28th, 1936 onwards (Weekdays)			
Time (Dep.)	From	Destination	Notes
12.4 a.m. SX	*11.58 p.m. Preston*	*L'Hall Carriage Sdgs.*	*Empty Stock*
5.23 a.m.	5.18 a.m. Preston	*Todmorden*	
5.35 a.m.	5.35 a.m. Preston Junction	Croston	Empty Stock Forms 6.0 a.m. to *Ormskirk*
6.20 a.m.	6.15 a.m. Preston	Blackburn	
6.35 a.m.	6.48 a.m. Preston	Blackburn	
7.11 a.m.	7.6 a.m. Preston	Liverpool Exchange	
7.15 a.m.	7.10 a.m. Preston	Wakefield	**9** (Reporting No.) Calls at Gregson Lane Halt
7.35 a.m.	7.30 a.m. Preston	Burscough Junction	
7.45 a.m.	6.33 Blackpool Central	Skipton	
8.4 a.m.	*8.0 a.m. Preston*	*Todmorden*	
8.8 a.m. SX	*8.4 a.m. Preston*	*L'Hall Carriage Sdgs.*	*Empty Stock*
8.12 a.m.	*8.8 a.m. Preston*	*Liverpool Exchange*	

September 28th, 1936 onwards (Weekdays)			
Time (Dep.)	From	Destination	Notes
8.1 p.m. SX	*7.57 p.m. Preston*	*L'Hall Carriage Sdgs.*	*Empty Stock*
8.2 p.m. SO	*7.30 p.m. Southport C.St.*	*Accrington*	*Express*
8.28 p.m.	8.23 p.m. Preston	Accrington	Formed by 7.30 p.m. from Blackpool North **SX**
8.47 p.m.	8.42 p.m. Preston	Ormskirk	
9.13 p.m.	8.10 p.m. Blackpool Central	Accrington	
9.18 p.m.	5.13 p.m. Penrith	Burscough Junction	**282** (Reporting No.)
9.43 p.m. SO	9.10 p.m. Southport	Todmorden	Express
10.9 p.m.	*9.15 p.m. Blackpool Central*	*Colne*	*Express*
10.17 p.m.	10.12 p.m. Preston	Accrington	
10.35 p.m. SX	10.30 p.m. Preston	Ormskirk	
10.40 p.m. SX	10.35 p.m. Preston	Blackburn	
11.0 p.m. SO	10.55 p.m. Preston	Liverpool Exchange	Express
11.3 p.m. SO	*11.0 p.m. Preston*	*Accrington*	
11.4 p.m. SX	11.0 p.m. Preston	Preston Junction	Arrives
11.15 p.m. SX	11.15 p.m. Preston Junction	Lostock Hall Shed	Light Engine
11.19 p.m. SO	11.15 p.m. Preston	Preston Junction	Arrives Empty Stock
11.25 p.m. SO	*11.20 p.m. Preston*	*Lostock Hall Shed*	*Light Engine*
11.30 p.m.	*11.25 p.m. Preston*	*Lostock Hall Shed*	*Light Engine*

Italic text shows passing times (non-stopping trains).
Rows shown shaded will turn West leaving Preston Junction towards Lostock Hall.

154

A view of the station from the road bridge in May 1968. *(Ivan Stewart)*

The all timber box which offered poor visibility for the signalman in the Preston direction. It might have been better had it been elevated above parapet level, as with the box at Lostock Hall Junction.
The former Stationmaster's house is partly obscured by the junction signals,
station name and timetable boards. *(Tom Wray)*

One of the BR Sugg pattern gas lamps receives attention from a maintenance man in 1968. This man is reputed to have come from the Cherry Tree district in Blackburn, and was the only remaining person to be employed on such work in the area. The formerly well-tended flower beds are now overgrown with weeds and the canopy shows signs of fire damage. On the embankment to the immediate left of the canopy, the station's name had once been visible in the form of white-washed stone blocks.
(Courtesy, Chris Canner)

Down Passenger Workings at Preston Junction

The table on the following page serves to illustrate typical passenger workings at Preston Junction, where the east and west workings combine. Most work to or through Preston, although any destined for Southport will fork west at Whitehouse South Junction and take the WL line. There are a few more interesting stock workings here: the 5.38 am. empty stock from Lostock Hall arrives at 5.42 am. and forms the 5.43 am. to Preston, followed by the 7.16 am. empty stock from Preston NU via Lostock

The junction layout as seen from the footplate of the same engine that brought us into the station.
Brownedge crossing can be seen just beyond the pre-1884 ticket platform and loop.
The LYR parachute water tank is the third one in the immediate area, the other two being located at each end and on opposite sides of the station platform. *(Alan Castle)*

Hall, which arrives at 7.46 am. and forms the 7.47 am. to Preston. Also of note are two light engine movements, which run 15 minutes earlier during the carriage heating season which, for express trains running in the late evening and early morning, was from the third Monday in September until May 31st; for other passenger trains it was from October 1st until May 31st.

Time (Dep.)	From	Destination	Notes
September 28th, 1936 onwards (Weekdays)			
2.24 a.m.(Junc.)	1.50 a.m. Liverpool Exchange	Preston	Express
5.25 a.m.	5.20 a.m. Lostock Hall Shed	Preston	Light Engine
5.43 a.m.	5.43 a.m. Preston Junction	Preston	see text
5.48 a.m. MX	5.43 a.m. Lostock Hall Shed	Preston	Light Engine
6.15 a.m. SX	6.10 a.m. Lostock Hall Shed	Preston	Light Engine - see text
6.30 a.m. SX	6.25 a.m. Lostock Hall Shed	Preston	Light Engine - see text
6.43 a.m.	6.0 a.m. Accrington	Preston	
6.52 a.m.	6.0 a.m. Liverpool Exchange	Blackpool Central	Express
7.22 a.m.	6.50 a.m. Ormskirk	Preston	
7.28 a.m.	7.3 a.m. Blackburn	Preston	Calls at Gregson Lane Halt
7.47 a.m.	7.47 a.m. Preston Junction	Preston	see text
8.35 a.m.	7.40 a.m. Burnley Bank Top	Preston	
8.49 a.m.	8.25 a.m. Burscough Junction	Preston	
9.2 a.m.	7.40 a.m. Colne	Preston	
9.36 a.m.	8.40 a.m. Liverpool Exchange	Blckpool North	
9.58 a.m.	9.7 a.m. Rose Grove	Preston	
10.8 a.m.	9.34 a.m. Accrington	Southport	Express calls at Bamber Bridge when required to take up passengers for Southport
10.19 a.m. SX	9.47 a.m Accrington	Blackpool Central	Express
10.19 a.m. SO	8.42 a.m. Halifax	Blackpool Central	Express
10.33 a.m. SO	7.57 a.m. Normanton	Blackpool Central	Express
10.33 a.m. SX	8.42 a.m. Halifax	Blackpool Central	Express
10.59 a.m.	10.55 a.m. Lostock Hall Shed	Preston	Light Engine
11.29 a.m. SX	10.12 a.m. Todmorden	Preston	
11.31 a.m. SO	10.12 a.m. Todmorden	Preston	Calls at Gregson Lane Halt
12.5 p.m.	11.10 a.m. Liverpool Exchange	Blackpool Central	
12.13 p.m.	11.33 a.m. Accrington	Preston	
12.39 a.m. SO	12.4 p.m. Accrington	Southport Chapel Street	
12.44 a.m.	11.21 a.m. Todmorden	Blackpool Central	Express SO
1.3 p.m. SO	12.40 p.m. Blackburn	Blackpool Central	
1.3 p.m. SX	12.40 p.m. Blackburn	Preston	
1.20 p.m.	12.27 p.m. Liverpool Exchange	Preston	Express
1.30 p.m. SO	11.48 a.m. Skipton	Blackpool Central	50 (Reporting No.) Express
1.44 p.m. SO	1.2 p.m. Padiham	Southport Chapel Street	
1.55 p.m.	12.32 p.m. Todmorden	Preston	
2.13 p.m. SO	1.40 p.m. Ormskirk	Preston	
2.37 p.m.	2.2 p.m. Accrington	Southport Chapel Street	Express
3.3 p.m. SX	2.27 p.m. Accrington	Preston	
3.10 p.m. SX	3.5 p.m. Lostock Hall Shed	Preston	Light Engine
3.11 p.m. SO	1.52 p.m. Todmorden	Preston	
3.20 p.m.	2.48 p.m. Ormskirk	Preston	
3.58 p.m.	2.36 p.m. Todmorden	Blackpool Central	

View from Brownedge Road bridge. Black 5, 45081 with self-weighing tender rounds the Preston Junction curve towards Lostock Hall Junction, with a Blackpool to Dundee seasonal extra train (as far as Carlisle) in the 1960's. *(Alan Castle)*

The following is a summary of a fairly well known accident at Preston Junction, the details have been taken directly from the board of trade report.

Collision August 3rd 1896 on the Lancashire & Yorkshire Railway at Preston Junction. The 8.10 am. West Lancashire Company's passenger train from Blackburn to Preston, headed by six-wheeled tender engine No 2, was approaching Preston Junction station at 8.46 am., when it collided with a LYR special train from Leeds to Blackpool, headed by engine No 1058, which was just moving out of the loop onto the main line.

One person, the Rev. R. J. Adams, was killed after being thrown from the carriage and having then been struck by a portion of the roof. A second man was badly injured and the train-men escaped without injury. After the collision the three rear vehicles were off the rails to the right. The sole cause was clearly a mistake made by the driver of the LYR excursion train, and driver Wigglesworth admitted his error without reservation. There were two signal arms in front of him: the higher one for the main line, having been off for 2 or 3 minutes and the lower one for the loop line, clearly distinguished by a ring on the arm, which remained at danger. He realised his mistake almost as soon as he had given his engine steam, but he was unable to prevent the collision which followed. They were on a falling gradient of 1 in 117 with a heavy train and would have been unable to stop at once. The question of safety-points on the loop line was mentioned by the coroner, and it seems probable that if there had been safety-points the excursion engine would have dropped off on to the ballast without further injury to anyone. This is a running loop, however, and facing safety points under such conditions would be likely to cause more accidents than they would prevent.

Visually, the position of the signal post at the end of the ticket platform was not satisfactory, being too close to the fouling point of the two lines, and it was recommended that steps should be taken to improve this, and where possible, signals for separate lines should be located on separate posts.[2]

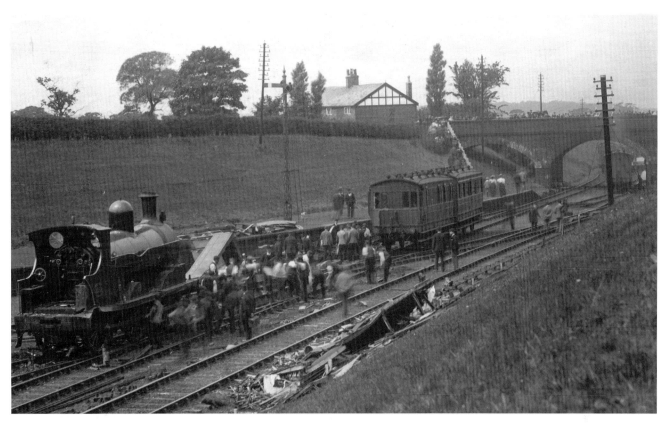

The scene of the 1896 accident looking north towards the station.
Note the large gathering of spectators on the bridge. *(British Railways)*

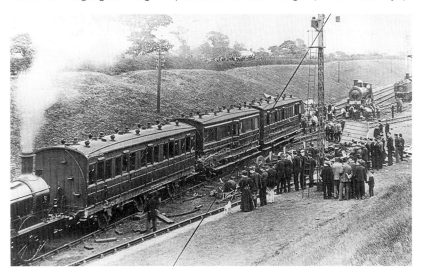

Another view of the wreckage from the bridge. People have gathered
on the old Preston platform for a closer look. *(British Railways)*

Brownedge Crossing

This was the site of the Preston Junction Level Crossing signal box, later called Brownedge Crossing (after the road). It was located on the Preston side of the road and, apart from the level crossing gates, it controlled entry to the Up Slow line towards Bamber Bridge and entry to the Down Loop (ticket platform) towards Preston Junction. The box was erected in 1904, having a brick base and timber superstructure, and was fitted with a 24 lever LYR frame. The former crossing keeper's cottage on the Bamber Bridge side of the road has been used as a private dwelling for many years.

Absolute block working was in force on all lines, and by 1969 the 'Up Slow' loop to Bamber Bridge had been noted as being signalled for passenger train working, but had no booked passenger train services on that loop. The box was taken out of use in 1972 with the commissioning of Preston PSB.

Crossing keeper's cottage and gates at Brownedge. *(Tom Wray)*

Level crossing box at Brownedge. *(Tom Wray)*

Bamber Bridge Junction & Exchange Sidings

The lines from Preston Junction and Lostock Hall converged at Bamber Bridge Junction. The first signal box here was originally on the station platform and was replaced in 1881 by a new Bamber Bridge Junction cabin of 48 levers, which controlled the goods yard, loop and sidings. The third cabin on the site dated from 1904 and was an all timber LYR design (size 18) with 84 levers, which controlled the up slow loop from Brownedge Crossing, the goods yard and access to the marshalling yard, as well as the main junction. All main lines were worked using absolute block.

The working of vehicles on running lines without a brake van in the rear (Rule 153) was authorised between Bamber Bridge Junction and Lostock Hall Engine Shed, on both up and down lines (20 loaded or 30 empty wagons).

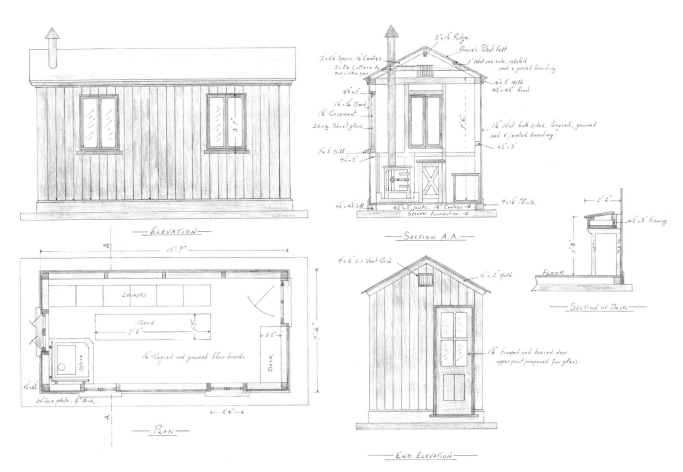

LYR plan & elevation drawing for shunter's cabin at Bamber Bridge Exchange Sidings.
(Drawings by author, taken from original LYR plans. Courtesy Greater Manchester County Records Office)

The old exchange sidings were situated on the south side of the line to Brownedge crossing, in the junction fork, and accessed via the up main line from Lostock Hall. Two of the seven roads ran parallel with the up-main, and the remainder ran likewise with the down main to Preston Junction.

The new exchange sidings, comprising twelve roads and a loop connecting with the up main to Blackburn, were built on the north side of the junction fork and terminated close to Brownedge Road. The station yard had a goods shed built of stone with two longitudinal gabled roofs. It was open-ended with a loading platform and jib-crane in the centre, and had two straight-through roads connected by wagon turn-tables at the east end. A ten ton yard crane was located between the tracks, just beyond the turn-tables. Edward Hopwood was the agent for the LYR carting services in 1889. There were stables for carting and shunting horses, a weigh bridge and extensive coal sidings on the south side of the yard. Coal merchants at the yard in 1898 included John Nelson, James Sumner (also cab proprietor), Thos. Hargreaves, Thos. Noblett, Thos. Walmsley; and the agent for the Wigan Coal & Iron Company was Moses Hunt. In 1887 the LYR agreed to the construction of a short branch line from a turn-back siding at the south-west end of the yard to Cuerden Mill, via a bridge over the old tram road, a distance of some 700 yards. As the line approached the north end of the mill, a spur curved away and entered the main works yard for the supply of coal to the engine house.

The branch line continued in a southward direction between the mill and workers cottages on Dewhurst Row, before reaching the main loading area. The mill had its own locomotive, an 0-4-0 saddle tank built by Peckett in 1892. It was painted in green livery and carried the name 'Monarch'. It served the works for many years, until its closure in 1934. The mill was owned by 'Geo. and R Dewhurst,' who also owned Higher Walton mill. In 1910, these two spinning mills had a total of 2,185 looms with 145,488 spindles and employed 2,030 hands. [3]

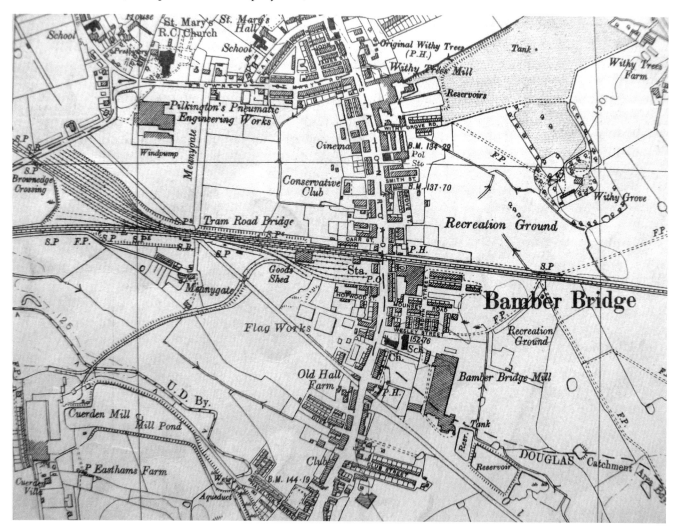

1896 map of Bamber Bridge, showing exchange sidings and branch to Cuerden Mill. *(Harris Library)*

The following is an account of the Cuerden Mill railway from the memoirs of Arthur Eric Crook, 1917 to 1997:

Dewhurst Row.

'The peculiar thing about our street, which set it apart from all others, was that a railway engine and wagons ran down the middle of it. Railway lines ran down the entire length of the street. A bridge had been built over the River Lostock and a railway track crossed the fields, then went into the goods yard at Bamber Bridge station. It was the factory's own private line. It saved a long haul by road, and all the wagons were loaded in the factory yard, so hundreds of tons went on one journey instead of the dozens of loads that would have had to go by motor or horse drawn vehicles.

Also, goods were brought back on the return journey. A man walked in front of the train with a red flag while it traversed the street itself, and shoved all the kids out of its path. I was only allowed to watch the proceedings by looking through the window. When the train whistle went at the start of its journey I had to dash home.'

The railway companies earned much revenue from the local mills, both in goods and in people. An extract from a Preston journal informs us of an excursion from Bamber Bridge to Morecambe via Hellifield, for workers at Cuerden Mill (always referred to by locals as Dewhurst Mill) and their families, totalling one thousand people on two trains, on Saturday, August 8th, 1891.

Freight Services at Bamber Bridge

These two Trip Workings for June 16 to October 5, 1947, which were unique to Bamber Bridge are included to complete the overall pattern of trip workings, with a separate analysis for a later period following.

No. 29 - BAMBER BRIDGE SHUNT Class 7 Freight Engine				
7.0 a.m. to 9.55 a.m. MO				
	dep. **MO**		arr. **MO**	dep. **MO**
	a.m.		a.m.	a.m.
Lostock Hall Shed	7.0 L.E.	Bamber Bridge	7.5	9.55 **A**
A - Works 10.0 a.m. To Normanton				

No. 9 - Class 7 Freight Engine (G.2.)		
6.20 a.m. MO to 6.0 a.m. Sundays		
Work as required to and from Preston Dock also works the following trips:		

(Engine to be facing South and sent to Shed at suitable time for coal)	arr.	dep.
	p.m.	p.m.
Preston Dock		11.40
		a.m.
N.U. Yard	11.50	12.2 **MX & Sun**
	a.m.	
Bamber Bridge	12.20	1.0 **MX & Sun**
Preston Dock	1.35	

Much of the traffic is similar to the 1947 insight at Butler Street, and it should be noted that most of the trip workings change direction at Bamber Bridge. As would be expected, most of the East Lancashire through workings are empty mineral trains returning to the colliery or other sorting sidings (for example Rose Grove or Healey Mills). It must be assumed that local coal empties would be marshalled into these trains here. In the down direction, the majority of traffic was for Lostock Hall, with most loaded workings simply passing through Bamber Bridge to Aintree Sorting Sidings and Wyre Dock.

The No 18 trip, which worked out to Hoghton at 9.00 am. and passed in the down direction at 9.32 am. was the Lostock Shunt and is stated in 1962 as: Class 4MT Tank (Ex LMS 2-6-2 T) 'Shunt and works trips as required, also work 11.0 am. Loco coal, Lostock Hall Sidings to Lostock Hall Shed'. [4] Therefore one can also assume some of the coal traffic at Lostock Hall was directly consumed by the engine shed, presumably working on an 'as needs' basis.

Bamber Bridge Station

The original station at Bamber Bridge was opened on June 1st 1846 by the Blackburn and Preston Railway, and served a community which owed much of its livelihood to cotton manufacturing. Several mills existed without direct rail access, including those of J. & A.S. Orr (School Lane Mill); Richard Aspen & Co.; William Eccles & Sons and, of course, the large 1907 mill of the Bamber Bridge Spinning & Weaving Co.[5]

Around 1885 the LYR made some improvements to the station, which included a new stone-built waiting room on the up platform; a subway crossing at the eastern end of the platforms, and the provision of new washroom facilities. The station was de-staffed in the mid- 1970's, the stone buildings being demolished shortly after, with the exception of the ticket office.

The original low-level stone platforms have been replaced by modern designs, and draughty bus shelters put in place. The subway has been filled-in, meaning pedestrians now have to wait if the barriers are lowered for the passage of a train. The signal box at Bamber Bridge is one of the few remaining original structures following the re-signalling at Preston.

The station signal box was originally located at the east end of the up platform and replaced on October 7, 1906 by the current 3-story timber LYR box, which housed a 12-lever frame and controlled the block section (absolute block) and crossing gates for the main A6 trunk road. Following the Preston

Just a Line from Bamber Bridge

A Postcard to prove that folks really did go to 'Brig'
for their holidays! *(Author's collection)*

Handbill and tickets
(Author's collection)

re-signalling, the lever frame was replaced by a 6-switch panel, and the gates replaced by full lifting barriers on 11th November, 1973. This box also controls the barriers at the Hospital and Mintholme crossings, using CCTV, and was renamed Bamber Bridge Level Crossing Frame. Between October 1972 and September 1973, as the Preston PSB re-signalling work was underway, it acted as the link up box between 'Preston Signal Box Stage 2' and 'East Lancashire Re-Signalling Stage A'. Today the line is signalled from Preston PSB using TCB.

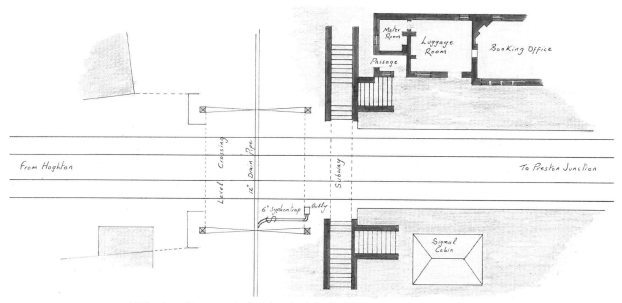

LYR plan: Proposed pipe for draining subway *(Author's collection)*

Bamber Bridge station looking east in 1906. *(Author's collection)*

In October 1907 the LYR introduced a motor bus service between Bamber Bridge and Chorley, with two 28h.p. Milnes-Daimler vehicles, to which Newton Heath added 34 seat bodies. They were formally used on the Blundellsands to Thornton route and their main purpose was to provide a feeder service to the railway; however, due to the poor state of the roads, they were frequently taken out of service for repairs. To address the problem, a third vehicle (a Commer) was acquired in March 1909, but this proved to be unnecessary as, shortly after, the company decided the service was uneconomical and it was completely withdrawn in October 1910, the first bus No B2084, being converted to a lorry. [6]

An interesting view of the station and goods shed from the footplate of 90675. *(Alan Castle)*

Stanier class 5, 44766 of Crewe South shed, thunders through the station
with a coal train for Fleetwood power station in the 1960's. *(Author's collection)*

The former L & Y Railway Hotel is situated next to the railway tracks in the north east corner of the level crossing, and the proprietor in 1881 was Thomas Eccles. Gillibrand's Railway Inn, which was commonly known as the 'Engine' in its heyday, is located a little further along Station Road on the south-east side of the crossing. In 1881 it was classified as a 'beer house' and the proprietor in that year was Mr. J. Webster. The former establishment had its name changed to the Lancs and Yorks in the 1980's and the latter now goes under the title of the Bamber Bridge Band Club. These two pubs were once quite convenient and popular watering-holes for the railwaymen, coalmen and carters.

An early 60's scene, with DMU pulling into the station on the Preston - Colne service.
Note the parcels on the platform ready for loading. *(D. J. Tomlinson)*

A view of the inside of Bamber Bridge Box *(Jeff Mimnagh)*

Hospital Crossing

Hospital crossing in the late 1800's. The crossing keeper's cottage
is the gabled building on the right. *(David Hunt)*

This site gets its name from the Hospital Inn, located opposite the level crossing, and there seem to be different tales as to why the inn is so named. Bradkirk House off Brindle Road was said to have been an isolation hospital, and the inn itself is reputed to have been a resting place for soldiers returning from the Crimean war, en route to the infirmary (presumably in Preston).

The signal box at this location was brick based with timber superstructure in an RSCo. style, housing a 12 lever frame. It was opened in 1883 as a block post (absolute block) and controlled the level crossing gates on Brindle Road. The box became a level crossing frame on September 23, 1973 when the Preston PSB took control of the line. The notice to drivers stated the actual switch over to the PSB as Monday September 28, 1973, when 'Stage A' went live. The box closed later that year when Bamber Bridge Level Crossing Frame took over. The crossing keeper's house still stands, and was formally rented by Frank Taylor, a long serving railway employee, who worked as a porter/ticket clerk further down the line at Penwortham Cop Lane Station.

Gregson Lane and Brindle Mill

This was the site of a small halt almost half a mile from the village of Gregson Lane, and was down a narrow lane called Bourne's Row. Gregson Lane itself hosted a mill in the centre of the village, but there was also another close to the railway called Hoghton Spinning & Manufacturing Co., which had its own private sidings.

The original plans show 'J & W Bourne Sidings', who were mentioned as owners of the mill on the list of Master cotton spinners and manufactures for 1882-1883. This also listed the mill as having 330 looms, 30,000 spindles, and employing 276 hands. There were two sidings, one for loading and unloading goods beneath the cover of a free-standing canopy, and the other for the supply of coal to the mill's engine house. The original Saxby & Farmer signal box dates from 1873. This was replaced circa 1950 with a LMS type brick based structure containing a 15 lever frame. It served as a block post (absolute block), controlling the level crossing and access to the mill. The box closed on December 8, 1961.

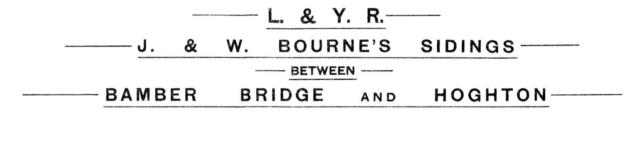

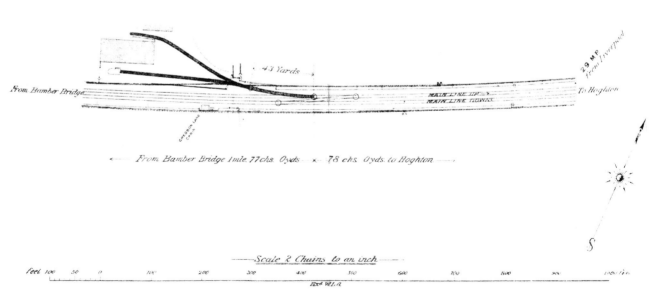

J & W Bourne's sidings diagram. *(Brindle Historical Society)*

Gregson Lane signal cabin and mill sidings in LMS days. *(Brindle Historical Society)*

Collision September 17, 1873 between a passenger train and a goods train at Gregson Lane siding near Hoghton station on the Lancashire & Yorkshire Railway. No injuries reported. The weather was misty and rainy. An Up Goods train from Liverpool to Blackburn consisting of a six-coupled engine with tender and 29 loaded wagons, had left Bamber Bridge Junction and was approaching Gregson Lane siding at 9.26 am. at a slow pace, due to the slippery state of the rails and the weight of the load. It had taken 14 minutes to travel 1 ½ miles! Close behind it was the 9.10 am. up fast train from Preston to Blackburn.The signalman at Gregson Lane sidings knew the down fast train from Blackburn to Liverpool was now due, but not in sight, so he stopped the goods train and sent it across on the down line, out of the way of the up passenger train.

The goods train set back through the points slowly and the greater part of the train had reached the down line, when the down passenger from Blackburn, travelling at about 40 m.p.h., approached the Gregson Lane distant signal, which was at danger. The driver whistled for the signal to be taken off and for the guards brakes to be applied. On seeing the obstruction ahead, he put his engine into reverse and the speed was reduced to about four or five miles per hour at the point of collision, which occurred at 9.28 am., upsetting two wagons. The engineman and fireman jumped clear.

'The driver of the passenger train was partially to blame as he had approached the down distant signal at so high a speed that he failed, though assisted by continuous brakes on six out of the eight vehicles, to stop at a point 625 yds. within that signal'.

'Secondly the signalman at Gregson Lane siding, knowing the down passenger train was due, should have waited longer than he did before allowing the goods train to cross, after putting his down signal to danger'.

'The signalman at Bamber Bridge junction is as much to blame for having allowed a fully loaded goods train to start up the gradient, only 10 minutes in front of a fast passenger train. If he had waited for the passenger train to pass, there was nothing to follow for a considerable time'. *'Had the traffic been worked using the absolute block system this collision would not have occurred. The Gregson Lane down distant should be moved at least 300 yards further from the home signal; 600 yards on a falling gradient of 1 in 100 is not sufficient distant for the protection of long goods trains'.* [7]

Passenger Services

These were somewhat strange: the following workings were booked to call at Gregson Lane and they are all shown in the Working Time Table as 'W.T.B. only' (Working Time Table Book), this possibly indicating they were for staff only, but they do not tie to the signal box opening hours, so could possibly be for mill workers as they seem to follow a normal 5½ day working week:

7.20 am. – 7.3 am. Blackburn to Preston
11.23 am. – 10.12 am. SO Todmorden to Preston (the SX service did not stop)
5.57 pm. – 4.18 pm. SX Rochdale to Blackpool North Express

7.24 am. – 7.10 am. Preston to Wakefield (Reporting No. 9)
11.52 am. – 11.38 am. Preston to Todmorden (calls Saturdays Only)
5.45 pm. – 5.32 pm. Preston to Accrington (calls Saturdays Excepted)

Freight Services

If the driver of a freight train needed to take water at a column on the main line, he was to give one long and three short whistles when passing certain points along the line. The information was then to be telephoned forward and control advised accordingly. Gregson Lane was one of those points for the requisition of water at Preston Junction or Lostock Hall (Preston EL was the point for the Up line).

There were two timetabled trip workings listed in the June 16th to October 5th 1947 trip working timetable: No. 24 and No. 26, the trip stopping on the outward leg to Hoghton. These provided an early Monday morning service (arr. 6.12 am. - dep. 6.31 am.) and a Saturday afternoon service (arr. 3.23 pm. – dep. 3.44 pm.).

Today an uncontrolled level crossing exists for farm traffic and the mill engine house is clearly visible with the main mill building behind. There is no evidence of the original halt or signal box.

Mintholme Crossing

Gregson Lane village is only a few hundred yards from this crossing and the lane running through the village and across the railway at this point is called Gregson Lane. The crossing itself was actually called 'Mintholme Crossing', presumable to avoid confusion with the halt 500 yds. down the line. Originally the crossing on Gregson Lane was operated from a crossing keeper's hut without a lever frame.

The site appears to have been equipped with a temporary frame or control panel when Preston PSB assumed control of the line on September 23rd 1973. The crossing is now controlled by barriers under the supervision of Bamber Bridge Level Crossing Frame.

Crossing keeper's cottage at Mintholme with small signal cabin on the right. *(Brindle Historical Society)*

Hoghton

The station at Hoghton was built in 1846, and being approximately half way between Blackburn and Preston, it marked the eastern limit of the Preston area. It was located adjacent to the main thoroughfare which is crossed on the level.

A goods yard with shed and facilities for the handling of coal were located on the north side of the station, and there were sidings on the south side for quarry traffic; there was also a down refuge siding to the east of the level crossing. The goods shed had a hand-operated jib crane, LYR No. 553, with 30 ft. of chain and 100 ft. of 7/8" diameter rope, to lift 25 CWT. There were two cranes in the yard: LYR No 737 hand-operated type with 48 ft of 15/16" chain to lift 5 tons, and a hand-operated lorry crane with 30 ft. of ½" chain, to lift 15 cwt.

Stone from the tower quarries was used for the construction of the buildings, as with the stations at Bamber Bridge, Pleasington and other structures in the area. The quarries were located on the north-east side of the tower knoll, where a narrow gauge railway operated on a gravity system, whereby

No. 24 - Class 3 Freight Engine					
	arr. **MO**	dep. **MO**		arr. **MX**	dep. **MX**
	a.m.	a.m.		a.m.	a.m.
Lostock Hall Shed		4.35 L.E.	Lostock Hall Shed		3.0 L.E.
Farington Jn.	4.40	5.0	Lostock Hall Sdgs.	3.5	3.20
Lostock Hall Sdgs.	5.5	5.30	Farington Jn.	3.26	4.10 L.E.
Bamber Bridge	5.36	6.6	Lostock Hall Sdgs.	4.15	4.55
Gregson Lane	6.12	6.31	Bamber Bridge	5.0	5.37
Hoghton	6.38	7.0 E&B	Hoghton	6.12	7.21 E&B
Bamber Bridge	7.8	7.26	Bamber Bridge	7.30	7.50
Lostock Hall Sdgs.	7.33	7.45	Lostock Hall Sdgs.	7.55	8.20
Farington Jn.	7.50	9.0	Farington Jn.	8.25	9.0
Lostock Hall Sdgs.	9.5	9.25	Lostock Hall Sdgs.	9.5	9.25
Bamber Bridge	9.32	9.50 L.E.	Bamber Bridge	9.32	9.50 L.E.
Lostock Hall Shed	9.55		Lostock Hall Shed	9.55	

No. 25 - Class 3 Freight Engine					
	arr. **SX**	dep. **SX**		arr. **SX**	dep. **SX**
	a.m.	a.m.		p.m.	p.m.
Lostock Hall Shed		6.0 L.E.	Lostock Hall Shed		3.0 **B**
Lostock Hall Sdgs.	6.5	11.10 **A**	Lostock Hall Sdgs.	3.5	3.27 L.E.
Preston (Butler St.)	11.24	11.55	Bamber Bridge	3.32	5.0 E&B
	p.m.	p.m.	Hoghton	5.7	5.45
Preston W.L.	12.10	12.45	Bamber Bridge	5.52	6.30
Lostock Hall Sdgs.	1.7	1.20 L.E.	Lostock Hall Sdgs.	6.35	7.5 L.E.
Lostock Hall Shed	1.25		Farington Jn.	7.10	8.40
			Lostock Hall Sdgs.	8.46	9.5
			Bamber Bridge	9.10	9.25 L.E.
			Lostock Hall Shed	9.30	

A - Shunts and makes trips as required between Lostock Hall Sidings and Bamber Bridge.
B - Loco. Coal Empties.

No. 26 - Class 3 Freight Engine					
	arr. **SX**	dep. **SX**		arr. **SO**	dep. **S)**
	p.m.	p.m.		p.m.	p.m.
Lostock Hall Shed		2.55 L.E.	Lostock Hall Shed		3.0 L.E.
Lostock Hall Sdgs.	3.0	**3.15**	Lostock Hall Sdgs.	3.5	3.10 E&B
Farington Jn.	3.20	4.0	Gregson Lane	3.23	3.44
Lostock Hall Sdgs.	4.8	4.28	Hoghton	3.52	4.35
Bamber Bridge	4.35	4.45 L.E.	Bamber Bridge	4.45	
Lostock Hall Shed	4.50 A		Bamber Bridge		5.0
Lostock Hall Shed		6.5 L.E.	Lostock Hall Sdgs.	5.5	5.20
Lostock Hall Sdgs.	6.10	6.25	Lostock Hall Shed	5.25	
Gas Works Sidings	6.35	7.18			
Bamber Bridge	7.48	8.0 L.E.			
Lostock Hall Shed	8.5				

A - Loco. Duties.

loaded wagons on the descent hauled up the empty ones with the aid of ropes and pulleys. The quarry sidings were controlled by a small signal box at Hoghton Tower crossing.

Hoghton station would have seen little in the way of day to day local passenger traffic, but there would have been a lot more activity during the wakes weeks, village outings, excursions and festive occasions. The tower buildings remained in a state of dereliction up to the commencement of restoration work in 1870 and Charles Dickens, who visited the site in 1854, described the Tudor-Elizabethan structure as being in 'A depressing state of disrepair'. These comments gave rise to renewed curiosity amongst the people of Lancashire and generated an eagerness to visit the place and learn more of its history.

An early photograph of the original station building at Hoghton.
A quarry wagon is parked in the foreground. *(Brindle Historical Society)*

The railway allowed these desires to be granted with ease and convenience, and the proprietor of the Railway Inn, [8] Mr. T.R. Thompson, had already placed an advert in local papers to the effect that, as the keys to the tower were in his possession, *'he will feel great pleasure in accompanying respectable parties desirous of seeing the interior of that time-honoured dwelling,'* and added: *'Dinners, Teas &c., provided on the shortest notice.'* [9] The station became particularly busy on Summer weekends with crowds of visitors,

Looking along the main thoroughfare towards the crossing in 1909. The extended goods shed is prominent in the left background. The rural serenity of this location has been spoiled by way of property development and the infernal combustion engine. *(Brindle Historical Society)*

172

all eager to look over the ancient buildings and enjoy the magnificent view afforded from the knoll, which is 560 feet above sea-level; with Mr. Thompson just as eagerly looking forward to guiding the folks back to his refreshment rooms.

Perhaps the busiest day of all time for the station was on Sunday, March 12, 1854, when tens of thousands of weavers and other mill operatives from Blackburn and Preston converged upon a field close to the station, which had been made available by Mr. Thompson free of charge.

This was a protest meeting arranged by the 'Wages Movement', whose organisers had been denied a venue in both of the industrial townships. Special trains had been ordered, and at 3 o'clock that afternoon, over 1000 people from Preston, equipped with their 'ten percent' flags and banners, arrived at the station. Mr. Thompson's establishment was overwhelmed, and the Police moved in and ordered everybody out amid uproar and much breakage of crockery and tankards. He was later charged with having his house open during a period of divine service, and was fined ten shillings. [10]

Structural changes were carried out in the 1890's by the LYR. The original stone station buildings were demolished, giving place to a less characteristic brick design, and the goods shed received an extension in brick with a lower roof level, the whole presenting an odd and ungainly appearance. A by-pass was constructed in 1936, to avoid the narrow village road and crossing gates. The 'New Road', as it is still referred to by locals, crosses the line at high level 100 yards to the east of the station site.

In 1845, a new consortium calling itself the Preston & Wyre Extension and Darwen Junction Railway, proposed the construction of a line from the Preston & Wyre Railway's terminus at Maudland to a junction with the Blackburn & Preston Railway at Hoghton Tower, thence along the B&P as far as Feniscliffe (between Cherry Tree and Mill Hill stations), and branching off to join the Blackburn, Bolton & Darwen Railway at or near Lower Darwen. The construction costs would have been phenomenal, and once the engineer's estimates had been submitted, nothing more was heard of the proposed venture.

The Station in 1900. It was always well maintained and adorned with flower beds and large planters here and there, with most of the work being carried out by local people right up to the end. *(Brindle Historical Society)*

The original Hoghton signal box dates from 1876, and was replaced on September 23rd 1900 by a standard brick base and timber structure of the LYR style with a 40 lever frame. Following the closure of Hoghton Tower and Pleasington signal boxes on September 12, 1926, Intermediate Block Signals (IBS) were added to cover the two sections in the up direction.

These allowed the long block to be split into additional sections without the need for intermediate signal boxes and without reducing traffic flow. They were initially of the semaphore type (Cherry Tree Junction controlled the IBS in the down direction to Pleasington). The Hoghton Tower IBS and the distant for Pleasington were automatically placed at danger by the passing of trains. The box controlled the main sections, level crossing gates, up and down goods yards and the down refuge siding. Working was by the absolute block system.

Hoghton box in the 1960's just prior to the station's closure. A post-mounted pair of LYR cast-iron warning signs can be seen to the right of the calling-on signals. *(Brindle Historical Society).*

The door has been left ajar to let in some fresh air on what appears to be a hot Summer's day. Electricity has taken over from coal and gas, and there is a Belfast sink with cold running water. The old Lanky telegraph instruments have been replaced by the BR Bakelite designs, but the Bobby's rocking chair most certainly dates back to the LYR days. *(Brindle Historical Society)*

Freight Services

Apart from passing freight traffic there were trip workings timetabled for Hoghton. These form part of a complex web of transfers along the line; details of these workings are shown in the following tables. As can be seen, goods for Hoghton would be delivered by 'Target 24' as this worked back to Bamber Bridge with engine and brake van (E&B), with any goods from Hoghton being taken on either 'Target 25' (weekdays) or 'Target 26' (Saturdays). These trip workings would perform any local shunting operations needed within the yards.

This 1950's photo shows a slight contrast to that of 1900. The platform lamps have been converted to electric power with swan-neck tops, upper-quadrant signals on a tubular steel post have been installed and new flower beds with whitewashed stone borders have been put in place. All this work would have gone some way to earning Hoghton a place in the 'Best Kept Station' award. *(Brindle Historical Society)*

The Station Master and his staff have plenty to smile about as they pose between a notice board and flower bed in the 1950's. I can only assume they did very well in the B.R. Best Kept Station award. *(Brindle Historical Society)*

The station closed to passenger traffic in September 1960 and the goods yard closed on January 1st 1962. Preston PSB took over signalling along the line with the box becoming a Level Crossing frame until February 1st, 1976, following installation of automatic barriers. The special notice for the re-signalling indicates the automatic half barriers (AHB) would be provided from September 28th 1973. The reason for this delay was due to the Hixon AHB accident on January 6th 1968, where the Manchester to Euston express, almost travelling at full speed, struck an articulated lorry carrying a 120 ton transformer which had been moving slowly over the crossing when the barriers descended. The result of this accident was a formal inquiry, the outcome of which was a confirmation of policy on automating level crossings, but with additional safeguards, causing delay (or cancellation in some cases) of the policy for several years. It should be pointed out here that the Hoghton AHB crossing was different in concept to the others on the line, as this crossing was fully automatic and not supervised from a signal box and until the final draft of the policy was known, the signal box supervised the crossing with some temporary locking to Preston PSB.

Hoghton Tower Crossing box, with quarry sidings on the right beyond the white gates.
(Brindle Historical Society)

FOOTNOTES

(1) Signal boxes on the L&YR Lines North East Lancashire. Chris Littleworth.

(2) Board of Trade Accident Report, 3rd August 1896. G.W. Addison Lieut. Col. R.E.

(3) List of Master Cotton Spinners and Manufacturers 1882083. Cotton Mills of Preston, T.E. Dickenson.

(4) Shunting engine & local trip notice. Preston Operating District. 10th September 1962 until further notice. LMR. British Railways.

(5) Cotton Mills of Preston. T.C. Dickenson.

(6) Lancashire & Yorkshire Miscellany 2. Noel Coates.

(7) Board of Trade Accident Report, 17th September 1873. C.S. Hutchinson Lieut. Vol. R.E.

(8) This public house is just a few yards up the road on the south-east side of the station site. It has also been known as the Railway Hotel and the Railway Tavern. It is currently called the Sirloin, after the much disputed knighting of a loin of beef by King James 1st in 1617, at Hoghton Tower. It is rumoured that the king was in a state of intoxication at the time, which could explain away a lot of odd things which have occurred in history, couldn't it?

(9) Preston Guardian, September 10th, 1853.

(10) ibid. March 25th, 1854.

Appendix

Ada Ashworth. Ingredients and Recipes for 'Bacon Butty Wagon'.

Ingredients for the midday meal:
Vegetables for 100 persons:
Potatoes 65 to 70 lbs
Onions 4lbs
Carrots 20lbs
Beetroot (cooked) 4lbs
Cabbage (raw) 5lbs
Peas (dry) 5lbs
Swedes 30lbs
Cabbage (cooked) 35lbs

Meat for 100 persons:
Roast joint 15lbs
Mince for shepherds pie 10lbs
Sausage or sausage meat 10lbs
Irish stew mutton 15lbs
Liver 12 lbs
Meat & vegetable pie 15lbs
Lancashire hot pot (meat) 15lbs

Stuffing for 100 persons:
Nat. breadcrumbs 5lbs
Onions or leeks 2lbs
Sage & seasoning 5lbs
Milk or stock 2 pints.

Gravy:
Flour ¾ lb
Margarine ½ lb
Stock 8 pints
Seasoning 8 pints.
Browning 8 pints
For sausage, bacon, bean and potato pie.

Pastry for 100 persons:
Oatmeal pastry:
Flour 5lbs
Oatmeal 2 ½ lbs
Margarine 1 ½ lbs
Cooking fat 1 ½ lbs
Salt 1 ½ lbs
Water 1 pint

Flour pastry:
Flour 6lbs
Oatmeal 3lbs
Or 9 lbs flour
Margarine 1 lb
Cooking fat 1 ½ lb
Salt.

Pastry for boiled Roly Poly pudding:
National flour 8lbs
Raw grated potatoes 2lbs
Fat or suet 2 lbs
Baking powder 2 tablespoons
Salt
Bread crumbs 3 lbs
Dried fruit 4 - 5 lbs
Sugar 1lb
Spread pastry strips with fruit & sugar & sprinkle with breadcrumbs. Tie in floured cloth and boil 2-3 hrs.
Serve custard

Ode to Dick Wilson by 'Singing' Tommy Miller.

Poetry on the railways was quite common and went on up to the time of privatisation in 1995. Some of the poems or ditties were short, and others took up a sheet of foolscap; some were complementary, and others were derogatory. Each one told a story about a colleague or a questionable state of affairs, and the following can be fairly described as the appraisal of a good mate, with a touch of satire, in good old Lancashire banter. The words here are written down exactly as they were penned by Lostock Hall engine driver, Tommy Miller, who was better known as 'Singing' Tommy Miller from the days when he serenaded his mates at the shed. He must have been quite a melodious singer otherwise, bearing his immediate critics in mind, he would have had a different title to his name.

Dick Wilson began his working life at Lostock Hall engine shed, and shortly after becoming a passed cleaner in 1942, he was transferred to a depot in the London area and left the railway in 1944. He tried his hand at several jobs, including colliery work, and returned to the railway in 1960, working in the Crewe area until home-sickness brought him back to Lostock Hall in the mid-60's.

He then worked as a shunter at Bamber Bridge yard until its closure in 1968. Dick then went on to Preston and became a passenger guard. He was later promoted to conductor guard and retired through ill health in 1986.

A sequence in the life of Richard. by Tommy Miller.

I pen this verse just like a bard,
About a former railway guard.
I hope these lines will raise a smile,
So please sit down and read a while.

This story takes you back a bit,
For once a time he worked In't pit.
From't pit to t'railway he did go,
Near to wheer he started years ago.

He didn't come back ter Lostock shed,
But t'dummy wrassled at brig instead.
At work he ne'er supped or ate,
But always seemed to keep his weight.

He must 'ave gobbled up at 'ome,
Or he'd 'ave bin just skin and boan.
Years passed by and dawned the day,
The sidings closed, I'm sad to say.

The sheds at Lostock had gone.
A better depot there was none.
But what did 'appen to our star lad?
A loving husband and a dad.

No train to shunt, no use for t'pole,
Was he to wind up on the dole?
An integration started then,
And down to Preston came the men.

Our hero now looking far dapper,
Became a travelling ticket snapper.
Instead of a pole he had a flag,
…Or was it two and a big guard's bag.

Twelve dets, his books and a metal lamp,
Enough to test a weightlifter champ.
This is the life for me, thought he,
As through the links he climbed with glee.

Then all at once: what a commotion!
'Conductor Guard' was his promotion.
The picture had changed, the grass grew,
Again, he formed part of an engine's crew.

Abbreviations

AHB - Automatic Half Barriers
B&PR - Blackburn & Preston Railway
BR - British Railways
BRB - British Railways Board
DCE - District Civil Engineers
EL - East Lancs. (Lancashire)
ELR - East Lancashire Railway
LO&PR - Liverpool, Ormskirk and Preston Railway
LMR - London Midland Region
LMS - London Midland and Scottish
LNWR - London & North Western Railway
LYR - Lancashire & Yorkshire Railway
MS&LR - Manchester, Sheffield & Lincolnshire Railway
NU - North Union
PSB - Power Signal Box
RSCo - Railway Signal Company
REC - Railway Executive Committee
ROF - Royal Ordnance Factory
TCB - Track Circuit Block
WL - West Lancs. (Lancashire)
WLR - West Lancashire Railway

Bibliography of Primary Sources

1881 – Barrett's Directory
1882 – Barrett's Directory
1898 – Barrett's Directory

H. W. Tyler, Capt., R.E. – Accident Report – 21st June 1864 (Board of Trade)
F. H. Rich Lieut.-Col., R.E. – Accident Report – 7th June, 1870 (Board of Trade)
C. S. Hutchinson Lieut.-Col. R.E. – Accident Report – 22nd May, 1872 (Board of Trade)
C. S. Hutchinson Lieut.-Col., R.E. – Accident Report – 17th September, 1873 (Board of Trade)
F. A. Marindin Major R.E. – Accident Report – 7th July, 1889 (Board of Trade)
G. W. Addison Lieut. Col., R.E. – Accident Report – 1st June, 1895 (Board of Trade)
G. W. Addison Lieut. Col., R.E. – Accident Report – 3rd August, 1896 (Board of Trade)
E. Druitt Major, R.E. Accident Report – 1st August, 1903 (Board of Trade)
E. Druitt, Lieut.-Col., R.E. – Accident Report – 30th November, 1907 (Board of Trade)
A. Mount Major R.E. – Railway Accidents – 25th September, 1920 (Ministry of Transport)
J. W. Pringle Colonel – Railway Accidents – 20th November, 1924 (Ministry of Transport)
C. A. Langley Brigadier – Railway Accidents – 13th May, 1950 (Ministry of Transport)

Inspectors Sketches - R J Rawlinson courtesy The Signalling Record Society
Loading of Passenger and Freight Trains – May 1st 1939 (London Midland and Scottish Railway.)
Particulars, Plans and Conditions of Sale of Valuable Freehold & Leasehold Properties – Bamber Bridge (LMS)
Plan of 'Maintenance and Working of Junction' May 1910 (Harris Museum)
Preston Numbering Plan NW69000076 – Regional S&T Engr's Dept (LMR – British Railways)
Preston Signal Box Stages A, B and C - Special Notice 1330G – (LMR – British Railways)
Preston Signal Box Stages 1 and 2 - Special Notice 1202G – (LMR – British Railways)

Sectional Appendix to the Working Time Tables Central Division March 1937 (LMS)
General Appendix to the Working Time Tables with Sectional Appendix Central Division March 1937 (LMS)
Sectional Appendix 'Central Lines' 1st October 1960 (British Railways)
Sectional Appendix to Working Time Tables 'Northern Section' June 1969 (LMR – British Railways)
Sectional Appendix 'Northern Section' November 1973 (British Railways)
Sectional Appendix 'Northern Section' November 1973 (British Railways)
Sectional Appendix 'Northern Section' December 1977 (British Railways)

Service of Trains 1st October 1896 until further notice (West Lancashire Railway)
Special Notices & Instructions 1895 (West Lancashire Railway)

Shunting Engine and Local Trip Notice – Preston Operating District June 16th to October 5th 1947 (LMS)
Shunting Engine and Local Trip Notice – Preston Operating District 10th September 1962 until further notice – (LMR – British Railways)
Shunting Engine and Local Trip Notice Preston 10th September 1962 until further notice (British Railways)

Working Time Table – Passenger Trains (Central Division) September 28th 1936, until further notice (LMS)
Working Time Table – Passenger Trains Preston E.L & Preston Jn. June 16th to October 5th 1947 (LMS)
Working Time Table – Passenger Trains (Central Division) 15th Jun to 13th Sep 1959 (LMR – British Railways)
Working Time Table – Freight Trains (Central Division) 13th June to September 1960 (LMR – British Railways)

AN 13/1141 (The National Archives)
AN 109/672 (The National Archives)
AN 109/673 (The National Archives)
MRQ1/48 (The National Archives)
MT6/1667/3 (The National Archives)
MT6/2491/2 (The National Archives)
MT6/405/11 (The National Archives)
MT6/9/110 - The National Archives
NPR 4203/21 (Cheshire and Chester Archives and Local studies)
RAIL 1053/53/56 (The National Archives)

Bibliography of Secondary Sources

Bamber Bridge station history plaque (The Lancashire and Yorkshire Railway Society)

Biddle, Gordon – The Railways Around Preston, An Historical Review (Foxline Publishing 1989 and 1992) ISBN 1-870119-05-3

Castle, Alan Steam The Grand Finale. Morton Media. ISBN 978-1-906167-10-3

Coates, Noel – Lancashire & Yorkshire Railway Miscellany 2 (Enanar Publications in association with The Lancashire & Yorkshire Railway Society 2006) ISBN 0-9553233-0-4

Collinge, A. K. (Chairman) Visit to Preston North Western Gas Works – Chairman's Day 3rd July 1954 (Institution of Gas Engineers)

Cotterall, J. E. – The West Lancashire Railway (The Oakwood Press 1982)

Dickinson T. C. – Cotton Mills of Preston (Carnegie Publishing Ltd. 2002) ISBN 1-85936-096-3

Elliott, F. and Richardson, D. – Platform 32 – The Journal of the Lancashire & Yorkshire Railway Society (Lancashire & Yorkshire Railway Society 1990) ISSN 0143-8875

Foster, Richard – An Introduction to Preston It's History, Railways and Signalling (LNWR Society 1998) ISBN 0-09515490-6-5

Gairns, J. F. - The Railway Magazine – No. 347 May 1926 (Tothill Press Ltd)

Hall, Stanley – Railway Detectives, 150 Years of the Railway Inspectorate (Ian Allan Ltd. 1990) ISBN 0-7110-1929-0

Hewitson, Anthony – History of Preston, in the Country of Lancaster (Chronicle 1883)

Hunt, David – History of Walton-le-Dale and Bamber Bridge (Carnegie Publishing Ltd. 1907) ISBN 1-85936-043-2

Johnston, Howard (Compiler) – Rail June 28 - July 10 1990 (EMAP National Publications Ltd 1990) ISSN 0953-4563

Littleworth, Chris – Signal Boxes on the Lancashire & Yorkshire Railway Lines: North East Lancashire (Signalling Record Society 2002) ISBN 1-873228-21-X

Rush, Robert W. – The East Lancashire Railway (The Oakwood Press 1983) ISBN 0-85361-295-1

Swift, John (collection) – British Railways Layout Plans of the 1950's – Volume 5: ex-Lancashire & Yorkshire Railway Lines in West Lancashire (Signalling Record Society 1992 and 2003) ISBN 1-873228-04-X

Stewart, Bert – On the Right Lines (Peter Watts Publishing 1982)

Taylor, Stuart – Journey by Excursion Train Return from Blackpool (Central) (Foxline Publishing) ISBN 1-870119-55-X

Taylor, Stuart – Journey by Excursion Train Return Southport via the West Lancashire Line Morecambe via Preston & Lancaster (Foxline Publishing) ISBN 1-870119-41-6

Holden, Bryan - The Long Haul. The life and times of the railway horse. J. A. Allen & Co. ISBN 0-85131-395-7

Chris Hawkins & George Reeve. LMS Engine Sheds, Vol. 3 The Lancashire & Yorkshire Railway. ISBN 0-906867-07

V.R Anderson & G.K. Fox. A Pictorial Record of L.M.S. Architecture. OPC. SBN 86093 083 1

Walker, Gilbert. Road and Rail an enquiry into the economics of competition and state control. George Allen and Unwin Limited. 1947.

Pratt, Edwin. A. Railways and Nationalisation. P. S. King & Son. 1908.

Beeching, Dr. Richard. The Reshaping of British Railways. HMSO British Railways Board, London, 1963.

Hindle, David John. All Station to Longridge. A history of the Preston to Longridge Railway. Amberley Publishing 2010. ISBN 978-I-4456-0200-4

Bonus photographs

Class 4F, 0-6-0, 44596, with high-sided tender, gassing up on February 16, 1963. (Tony Gillett)

The ill-fated Britannia pacific, 70017 Arrow, looking presentable on August 14, 1962. (Tony Gillett)

Fowler 4MT, 2-6-4 tank.42319, contributes to the smog on february 16, 1963. (Tony Gillett)

Stanier tank, 42436, passes the Lostock Hall shed with a train for Liverpool in the mid-60's. (Stan Withers)

Above: One of the Patriot class locos that didn't carry a name, 45550, is ready for action on August 29, 1962. *(Tony Gillett)*

Below: Ex- Carnforth black 5, 44894, at Lostock Hall shed on April 19, 1969. This was the last steam loco to be removed from the shed, and it is rumoured that the reason for its long delay was that B.R. had offered her to the governing body at Lostock Hall School on Todd Lane, as a memorial to the town's railway heritage. Unfortunately, this offer was rejected on grounds of safety and cost of maintenance etc.. *(Author)*

Left: Swindon built 8F, 48476, on July 30, 1968. *(Author)*

Below: Big 8, 48775, shunts container wagons at Lostock Hall station on July 30, 1968. *(C.Stacey/Initial)*

Above: Redundant Jinties at Lostock Hall on August 20, 1963. Post-grouping, 47360, with ex-Midland 47211 behind her on road 10. Another pre-grouped 47201, minus her condensing pipe is on road 9. Note the two-wheeled hand cart adjacent to the goods van on road 9, and the rows of sleepers either side of road 10 which provided a base for the coal stacks. *(B.W.L. Brooksbank/Initial)*

Arriving on time in Spring 2012!

'The London and North Western Railway around Preston'

Another work by the same author, this time covering the 'North Union' section of the railway system around Preston, including the engine shed, station, goods sheds, dock branch, Maudland, Dock Street and the canal basin. We have included two pages here with samples of some of the pictures.

Tony Gillett

Tony Gillett

Tony Gillett

Stan Withers

H Gordon Tidy

Tony Gillett

Jack Hodgkinson